1 Aa An

Young People's Science Encyclopedia

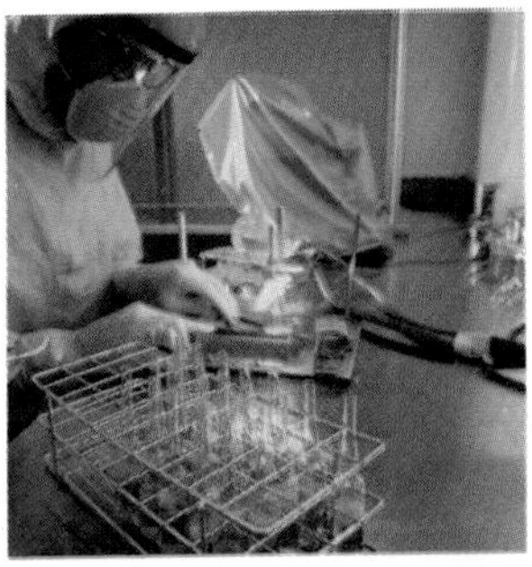

a

rdvark
rdwolf

b

alone
domen
ortion
rasives
solute zero
sorption, physiological
sorption of light

c

celeration
celerator
celerators
climatization
commodation
cetic acid
cetone
cetylene
cids and bases
cne
coustic weapons
coustics
cquired Immune Deficiency Syndrome (AIDS)
cromegaly
ctinide elements
ctinium

d

daptation
Addiction
Adding machine
Addison's disease
Adenoids
Adhesion
Adhesive
Adolescence
Adrenal glands
Adrenalin
Adsorption

Ae

Aerobic
Aerodynamics
Aeronautics
Aerosol
Aerospace

Af

Africa
Afterburner

Ag

Agassiz, Louis
Agate
Ageratum
Aging
Agriculture
Agronomy

Ai

Air
Air conditioning
Air hammer
Air lock
Air masses
Air pollution
Air pressure
Air resistance
Aircraft
Air-cushion vehicles
Airplane
Airships

Al

Albatross
Albino
Albumin
Alchemy
Alcohol
Alewife
Alfalfa
Algae
Algebra
Alimentary canal
Alkali deposits
Allergy
Alligator
Alloy
Allspice
Almond
Alpaca
Alpha
Alternation of generations
Altimeter
Altitude
Alum
Aluminum
Alyssum

Am

Amaryllis
Amber
Ameba
Ameboid movement
Americium
Amethyst
Amino acid
Ammeter
Ammonia
Ampere
Ampèré, André Marie
Amphibians
Amundsen, Roald
Amylase

An

Anatomy
Anchovy
Androgen
Anemia
Anemometer
Anesthetics
Angiosperms
Anhydride
Animal
Animal behavior
Animal cages
Animal diseases
Animal husbandry
Animal intelligence
Animal tracks
Animals, classification of
Animals, life span

National College of Education has been a leader in preparing teachers since it was founded as a kindergarten training institute in 1886. Today it has campuses in Chicago, Evanston, and Naperville, Illinois, with undergraduate and graduate programs in most educational fields. Teachers and school administrators trained at the National College of Education now work throughout the United States and in many other countries. In addition, the college provides in-service training, consultation, and workshops to professional educators. Its centers in economic and career education, reading, special education, and science curriculum improvement are valuable resources for teachers and children.

Children are the focus of all educational programs at National College. The college has its own Demonstration School with nursery through eighth grade classes. Demonstration School teachers are talented and innovative practitioners who continue to improve the quality of education for the school's children in a setting where the college's student teachers, researchers, and observers may work with the children and study educational theories in action.

When *The Young People's Science Encyclopedia* was initially published in 1962, it was the first publication of its kind. National College is proud of its faculty who created this encyclopedia that has helped so many children increase their understanding of science. We hope that this new edition will continue to provide enjoyment and knowledge to children everywhere.

Orley R. Herron, President
National College of Education

Young People's SCIENCE Encyclopedia

Edited by the Staff of

NATIONAL COLLEGE OF EDUCATION
Evanston, Illinois

Volume 1/A-An

CHILDRENS PRESS ™
CHICAGO

Photographs

Page 2: Skylab space station (NASA)

Page 3: *Top to bottom:*
Wheatfield (U.S.D.A. Photo)
Technician capping Abbokinase (Abbott Laboratories)
Spider (Macmillan Science Company)
View of Earth (NASA)
Space Shuttle (NASA)
Bahama coral reef (Macmillan Science Company)

Cover: Rocket lift-off (NASA)
Lion (San Diego Zoo)
Butterfly (James Rowan)

Library of Congress Catalog Card Number: 67-17925

YOUNG PEOPLE'S SCIENCE ENCYCLOPEDIA

Edited by the Staff of
NATIONAL COLLEGE OF EDUCATION, Evanston, Illinois

CONTRIBUTORS

D.J.A. Donnalois J. Ahlstedt, B.Ed., M.Ed., formerly, Oakton School, Evanston, Illinois.

J.F.B. Jean F. Blashfield, B.A., Free-lance editor.

P.G.B. Phyllis G. Blodgett. Free-lance writer for *Reader's Digest: Christian Science Monitor.*

D.A.B. Donald A. Boyer, B.S., M.S., Ph.D., Science, National College of Education, Evanston, Illinois; Science Education Consultant, Winnetka Public Schools, Winnetka, Illinois.

M.R.B. Mary R. Boyer, B.A., M.Ed., D.B., Junior High School Coordinator, Winnetka Congregational Church.

J.D.B. Jacqueline D. Boynton, B.A., formerly, Science, Wilmette Junior High School, Wilmette, Illinois

E.R.B. Elizabeth R. Brandt, B.A., M.Ed., Science, National College of Education, Evanston, Illinois.

J.M.C. Jocelyn M. Cain, B.A., Free-lance writer for *Extension Datebook Christian Science Monitor.*

J.A.C. J. Allen Carpenter, B.A., Editor and Publisher, Carpenter Publishing House; Founder, *Teacher's Digest.*

H.J.C. Helen J. Challand, B.E., M.A., Ph.D., Chairman, Division of Natural Sciences, National College of Education, Evanston, Illinois.

R.S.C. Richard S. Clarke, B.S., Science, Wilmette Junior High School, Wilmette, Illinois.

M.B.C. Miller B. Clarkson, A.B., M.S., Science, Northeastern Illinois State College, Chicago, Illinois.

C.K.C. Calvin K. Claus, B.A., M.S., Ph.D., Psychology, National College of Education, Evanston, Illinois.

M.W.C. Martha W. Clausen, B.A., M.S., Demonstration School, National College of Education, Evanston, Illinois.

B.J.C. Bettie Jane Colwell, R.N., School and Office Nurse, Wilmette, Illinois.

J.H.D. John H. Daugherty, B.S., M.A., formerly, Science National College of Education, Evanston, Illinois.

J.A.D. Joan A. DeLapp, B.A., M.Ed., Northbrook Public Schools, Northbrook, Illinois.

D.L.D. Doralee L. Denenberg, A.B., formerly, Atomic Energy Commission; Assistant Mathematics Editor, Laidlaw Brothers, Publishers, River Forest, Illinois.

E.L.D. Earle L. Denenberg, B.I.E., M.S., Industrial Engineer, Johnson and Johnson, Chicago, Illinois

G.A.D. Gwendolyn A. DuBose, B.A., M.A., Doolittle School, Chicago, Illinois.

D.D. Don Dwiggins, Aviation Editor, Los Angeles *Daily News* and *Mirror News*, children's book author, reporter, commercial pilot, flight instructor.

K.A.E. Krafft A. Ehricke, B.A.E., H.L.D., Assistant Division Director, Astrionics Division, Autonetics, A Division of North American Aviation, Inc., California.

M.D.F. Margaret D. Feigley, B.S., M.A., formerly, Instructor in Biology at Harris Teachers College in St. Louis, Missouri.

I.K.F. Irwin K. Feinstein, B.S., M.A., Ph.D., Mathematics, National College of Education, Evanston, Illinois; University of Illinois.

H.S.G. Hal S. Galbreath, B.S., M.S., Science, National College of Education, Evanston, Illinois.

B.B.G. Beatrice B. Garber, A.B., M.S., Ph.D., formerly, Science, National College of Education, Evanston, Illinois.

B.M.H. Benjamin M. Hair, A.B., M.D., Courtesy Staff, Evanston Hospital, Evanston, Illinois; Clinical Assistant Professor, Preventive Medicine, University of Illinois; Private Practice, Internal Medicine.

A.J.H. Arthur J. Hannah, B.S., M.Ed., Ed.D., Chairman, Mathematics-Science Department, National College of Education, Evanston, Illinois.

D.C.H. Douglas C. Huffmon, B.Ed., Doolittle School, Chicago, Illinois.

D.J.I. David J. Itzov, B.A., M.A., Principal, Lake Bluff Junior High School, Lake Bluff, Illinois.

V.B.I. Violet B. Izard, B.A., M.A., formerly, Demonstration School, National College of Education, Evanston, Illinois.

C.B.J. Charles B. Johnson, B.S., M.A., M.S., Senior Meteorologist, United States Weather Bureau, Chicago, Illinois.

D.H.J. Dorothy H. Johnson, B.S., A.B., M.A., formerly, Demonstration School, National College of Education, Evanston, Illinois.

R.J.J. Raymond J. Johnson, B.B.A., M.Ed., Executive Officer, Civil Air Patrol Division, Illinois State Department of Aeronautics, Chicago, Illinois.

R.N.J. Richard N. Johnson, A.B., B.D., Ph.D., formerly, Psychology, National College of Education, Evanston, Illinois.

M.W.K. Marvin W. Keith, B.S., Project Engineer, General Time Corporation, Skokie, Illinois.

J.K.K. Jean K. Kendall, B.S., Radio and Television Writer, Ruthrauff and Ryan, Chicago, Illinois.

C.L.K. Carole L. Kidder, B.A., M.A., English, National College of Education, Evanston, Illinois.

E.Y.K. Elliot Y. Koyanagi, B.A., M.Ed., University School, Indiana University, Bloomington, Indiana.

J.C.K. Jean C. Kraft, B.S., M.A., Ph.D., Science, National College of Education, Evanston, Illinois.

W.J.K. Wanda J. Kuberski, B.A., Curriculum Consultant for Head Start Program, Chicago, Illinois.

J.K.L. Judith K. LaRoy, B.A., formerly, Biology, Skiles Junior High School, Evanston, Illinois.

M.I.L. Mildred I. Lavizzo, B.S., M.A., R.N., Public School Health, Chicago Board of Education, Chicago, Illinois.

A.E.L. Allen E. Lentz, B.S., M.A., Assistant Director of Research, Master Builders Research Laboratories, Cleveland, Ohio.

E.P.L. Elsie P. Lerman, B.A., B.F.A., M.F.A., Art, National College of Education, Evanston, Illinois.

M.R.L. Margaret R. Lindman, B.Ed., M.A., Principal, College Hill School, Evanston, Illinois.

M.M.L. Mary M. Lindquist, B.A., M.A., Ph.D., Mathematics, National College of Education, Evanston, Illinois.

H.W.M. Helen W. MacKinnon, B.A., M.Ed., Spectroscopy, formerly, Massachusetts Institute of Technology; formerly, Demonstration School, National College of Education, Evanston, Illinois.

L.M. Ludolph Martin, B.S., Science Coordinator, Libertyville, Illinois.

A.P.M. Avis P. Moore, B.A., M.A., Social Science, National College of Education, Evanston, Illinois.

E.M.N. Eileen M. Nelson, B.Ed., M.Ed., formerly, Education, National College of Education, Evanston, Illinois.

V.V.N. Virgil V. Nutt, B.S., M.S., Science Consultant for the Gifted Child Project, School District #65, Evanston, Illinois.

H.P.O. Harold P. Owen, B.S., Civil Engineering, Free-lance Writer (Physical Sciences and Technology).

M.S.P. Marvin S. Paul, B.S., M.A., Science, Loop College, Chicago, Illinois.

C.F.R. Charles F. Rockey, B.S., Science, New Trier High School, Winnetka, Illinois.

H.K.S. H. Kenneth Scatliff, M.D., Radiology, Ravenswood Hospital, Chicago, Illinois; Past President, Chicago Medical Society.

E.S.S. Eleanor S. Segal, M.D., Attending Staff, Cook County Hospital; Hospital Instructor, Department of Community and Preventative Medicine, Northwestern University Medical School, Chicago, Illinois.

I.H.S. Ida H. Simmons, A.B., M.A., Education, National College of Education, Evanston, Illinois.

P.P.S. Paul P. Sipiera, B.A., M.S., Geology and Physical Science, William Rainey Harper College, Palatine, Illinois; Research Associate, Field Museum of Natural History, Chicago, Illinois.

E.M.S. Essie M. Smith, B.A., M.S., Scientific Art; formerly, United States Bureau of Mines.

R.C.S. Ray C. Soliday, B.A., B.S., M.A., (Deceased), Nuclear physics, Oak Park-River Forest High School, River Forest, Illinois; Consultant, Argonne National Laboratories, Argonne, Illinois.

M.S. Marshall Sorkin, B.S., M.S., Research and Development Group Leader, Helene Curtis Industries, Inc., Chicago, Illinois.

J.R.S. Jesse R. Swoap, B.S., M.S., Science, New Trier High School, Winnetka, Illinois.

B.A.T. Bruce Allen Thale, B.S.Ed., M.S.Ed., Science, National College of Education, Evanston, Illinois.

F.R.W. Fred R. Wilkin, Jr., B.S., M.Ed., Science, National College of Education, Evanston, Illinois.

MAJOR ART CONTRIBUTORS

Argonne National Laboratory
Chicago Natural History Museum
Civil Air Patrol
Denoyer-Geppert Company
Environmental Science Services Administration
International Visual Educational Service, Inc.
Macmillan Science Company
National Aeronautics and Space Administration
National Teaching Aids, Inc.
Society for Visual Education, Inc.

FOREWORD

Young people all over the world are showing an active interest in science. They have a continuous need for up-to-date scientific information covering all of the topics they may encounter in daily life and in their studies. The YOUNG PEOPLE'S SCIENCE ENCYCLOPEDIA is a comprehensive reference work, produced in response to the needs of these young people. It is designed to include the science concepts taught in elementary and junior high schools.

This encyclopedia was developed to appeal especially to young people from the third through the ninth grades. The content was planned, however, with an even broader interest range. The editors estimate this range to be about nine years. This means that even advanced second graders can profit from some of the material in this set. Young people in high school can use the more technical and complex material.

The nearly four thousand topics covered in the YOUNG PEOPLE'S SCIENCE ENCYCLOPEDIA are drawn from all of the basic biological and physical sciences, as well as from many specialized branches from which elementary and junior high school science concepts are drawn. These special branches include aerodynamics, astronautics, electronics, medicine, meteorology, nuclear science, radiology, and many others. The YOUNG PEOPLE'S SCIENCE ENCYCLOPEDIA does not confine its coverage to practical information alone. Also included are more than two hundred THINGS TO DO which are placed near the informative articles to which they are related. Just as science is not limited to the study of information, this encyclopedia emphasizes not only the "look it up" approach but also "learning by doing."

OBJECTIVES OF THE ENCYCLOPEDIA

1. To provide the most convenient means to encourage young people in pursuing their interest in science;
2. To provide help for the young person in his schoolwork;
3. To involve the young person in learning by experimenting;
4. To provide a wide vocabulary and concept range to satisfy differing ages and abilities;
5. To provide parents and teachers with a ready means of helping young people in the area of science.

ORGANIZATION OF THE ENCYCLOPEDIA

The YOUNG PEOPLE'S SCIENCE ENCYCLOPEDIA was produced at National College of Education, Evanston, Illinois, as an educational project in cooperation with Childrens Press. The College has a long history of excellence in promoting elementary and junior high school education. The philosophy of education held by the staff of the College had a significant effect on the planning of the encyclopedia. To conceive, plan, and edit the encyclopedia the College brought together some of the best minds in the scientific world and in the fields of science and elementary education.

Most of the encyclopedia was written by classroom science teachers. Consulting editors also contributed articles from their own technical fields. These consulting editors represent such professional positions as college science teachers, science curriculum directors or supervisors teaching in public schools, industrial experts, consultants to United States government space and nuclear science programs, along with a professional meteorologist, a doctor of medicine, and a high official of the Civil Air Patrol. Other consulting editors represent the fields of reading and vocabulary control, English composition, and phonetics.

The editorial staff of the encyclopedia selected appropriate, colorful illustrations in consultation with curriculum specialists. There are photographs, maps, charts, diagrams, and artists' original drawings. These illustration materials come from the government, industries, educational societies, and publishers. Much original artwork was produced especially for this encyclopedia. The illustrations and informative captions help to tell the vivid story of science. Even children with severe reading handicaps can learn much from the illustrations. The high interest value of the artwork alone may motivate such children to improve their reading skills.

Split-level vocabulary

The articles of the encyclopedia were written with an easy-to-difficult sequence of concepts and vocabulary. Each article begins with basic and introductory facts printed in larger type, and gradually works into the more advanced technical concepts which are printed in smaller type. Depending on the technical difficulty of the entry, the beginning paragraph or paragraphs are scaled to about a third grade reading level.

The longer and more complex articles have a vocabulary and concept range from about the third through the ninth grade. Such a range obviously makes this reference set useful to young people for most of their school years. Moreover, such a range gives the intellectually gifted boy or girl a chance for more advanced learning. Frequently, science books of a specific lower grade level may be much too simple for them. This encyclopedia gives each young person an opportunity to progress at his own pace.

Alphabetical arrangement

The topics in the YOUNG PEOPLE'S SCIENCE ENCYCLOPEDIA are in alphabetical order. Compound words such as **Aircraft** come after terms such as **Air hammer**, thus keeping all entries beginning with the separate word "air" together. Plural titles are used when the subject discussed is plural: **Ants** instead of **Ant**. Complex topics may be broken into several entries and both the singular and plural forms are used. For example, **Animal** (a general introductory article) can be broken into **Animal cages**, **Animal diseases**,, **Animal husbandry**, **Animal tracks**, and **Animals, classification of** (the last, a more technical article).

Spellings and pronunciation

Modern spellings are used throughout the encyclopedia. For example, **Ameba** is used instead of **Amoeba**, **Esophagus** instead of **Oesophagus**. If pronunciation of an entry title is necessary, it follows the title in parentheses. No separate pronunciation key is needed since a phonetic use of the English alphabet is employed rather than the symbols of the International Phonetic Alphabet or diacritical marks. The accented syllables are in capital letters. Examples are **Abalone** (abb-uh-LOW-nee), **Ebony** (EBB-uh-nee), and **Camellia** (kuh-MEEL-yuh).

Cross-references

A topic may be included in alphabetical order only as a cross-reference, such as **Dromedary** see **Camel.**. The reader may be interested initially only in the dromedary. The cross-reference will lead the reader to discover immediately the relationships between this animal and its family. This will, in turn, interest him in continuing his study beyond his initial quest. Within articles, topics may be mentioned that are more fully discussed elsewhere in the encyclopedia. A term within an article that can be cross-referred is set in small capital letters to indicate the cross-reference. Again, such cross-references may lure the youth into relationships and more advanced study. Still other cross-references are given at the end of many articles. At the end of the entry on **Amino acid** is the cross-reference SEE ALSO: METABOLISM.

Format of the Encyclopedia

The format used in the YOUNG PEOPLE'S SCIENCE ENCYCLOPEDIA was planned to facilitate reading and to aid in the speedy location of desired information. In the longer articles, section headings are centered on the page column in small capital letters.

The articles on the various continents, for instance, are divided into five main sections for ready reference: LAND FORMS, WEATHER AND CLIMATE, RIVERS AND DRAINAGE, PLANTS AND ANIMALS, and NATURAL RESOURCES. If the young person wants information on the animals of Africa, he may skim through the article on that continent to the section on PLANTS AND ANIMALS without having to read through the whole article.

There are four uses for italics throughout the books of the encyclopedia: (1) within an article when a new concept or term is introduced for the first time; (2) within an article as a part of, a division of, or an example of the subject; (3) within an article as a subheading followed by a colon; and (4) to show that a word is from Latin or another foreign language.

Actual scientific names, expecially the phyla names of the plant and animal kingdoms, are sometimes used as topic titles while the more common or popular names are used in the text of the articles. For example, **Mollusca** is a title; within the article this family is called "mollusks." However, in some instances the scientific name is a part of a larger whole which may have a common or popular name. For instance, **Igneous** is cross-referenced to the major article on **Rocks. Femur** is cross-referenced to **Skeleton** because the femur is a part of the skeleton.

The initials at the end of all articles except straight definition articles are those of the writer. For the full name of the writer, refer to the list of contributors after the title page of Volume 1. All uninitialed THINGS TO DO were prepared by Dr. Helen Challand, Associate Editor. The PARENT AND TEACHER'S GUIDE, available as Volume 20, was prepared by the editors.

Above all, the encyclopedia presents an unmatched opportunity for exciting discovery. Its use can lead to intellectual growth and to improved reasoning powers. Science promotes honesty of reporting. It develops a healthy skepticism and prevents a jump to hasty and faulty conclusions. Its side effects are open-mindedness, fairness, and respect for things of proven worth. Most important, science provides a way of arriving at decisions after examining the best evidence available. YOUNG PEOPLE'S SCIENCE ENCYCLOPEDIA is dedicated to science as a way of life.

Evanston, Illinois National College of Education

San Diego Zoo

Aardvark (ARD-vark) The aardvark is an African MAMMAL 5 to 6 feet long (1.5 to 1.8 meters), weighing about 100 pounds (45 kilograms). Its Dutch name means "earth pig," but only its snout is pig-like. It has a body like a bear, ears like a donkey, a tongue like an anteater, and a tail like a kangaroo.

This animal is a nocturnal feeder. Even in a zoo, it arouses little interest among the visitors because it sleeps all day. In nature it lives in an underground burrow. This habit is also its defense, since it can dig a burrow faster than man can dig with a spade.

Because the aardvark lives mainly on a diet of destructive termites, this fascinating animal is valuable to Central Africa.

No other mammal has teeth like the aardvark. They are peglike without enamel. There are many milk teeth but only about five permanent teeth in each jaw.

Because of its hooflike nails, it is often said to be a descendant of the earliest hoofed mammals. Its fossil record dates back to the Miocene Period. D. H. J.

Aardwolf The aardwolf is an African MAMMAL in the same family as the HYENAS. It has the same human-like laugh, large head, and doggish appearance as the hyena. The front legs are larger and better developed than the rear ones. It is smaller and milder tempered than the hyena. Unlike the hyena, the aardwolf has weak jaws and small teeth. It eats termites and other insects rather than bones and flesh of larger animals.

Aardwolf means earth wolf. It is not a wolf but does live in holes. The fur is gray or yellowish with brown stripes on its back. When disturbed the mane along its back is erected and it gives off an odor. J. C. K.

Abaca see Hemp

Abacus see Computer

Abalone (abb-uh-LOW-nee) Abalone is a large saltwater shellfish or MOLLUSK. Its common name is ear shell. As in snails, there is only one shell. The spiral of the shell is flattened. Four or more openings on the shell edge are gill holes. The shell outside is rough, the inside smooth with many colors. Its flesh can be eaten.

Abalones live in salt water, some species at greater than 50 foot (15 meter) depths, others along shores at tide level. Each animal has its home rock where it settles by day but creeps about in search of seaweed by night. Zoologists are still trying to learn where and how abalone eggs are laid.

Various species occur in the Atlantic and Pacific oceans. The *red abalones* of California coasts have been so ruthlessly captured for their flesh and mother-of-pearl shells that laws have been passed forbidding capture except when the animals reach full size. The *European abalones,* once common along the shores of the English Channel islands, are now nearly extinct. D.A.B.

SEE ALSO: MOLLUSCA, PEARL

Abdomen (ABB-do-men) The abdomen is the large cavity in the middle of the body. It holds the stomach, the intestines and some of the reproductive organs. The large muscle called the *diaphragm* separates the abdomen from the thorax, or chest. The lower region is bounded by a layer of tissues which line the cavity of the pelvis. The abdomen is bounded in front by strong muscles popularly thought of as the stomach muscles and in the back by the vertebrae of the spine and the muscles of the back.

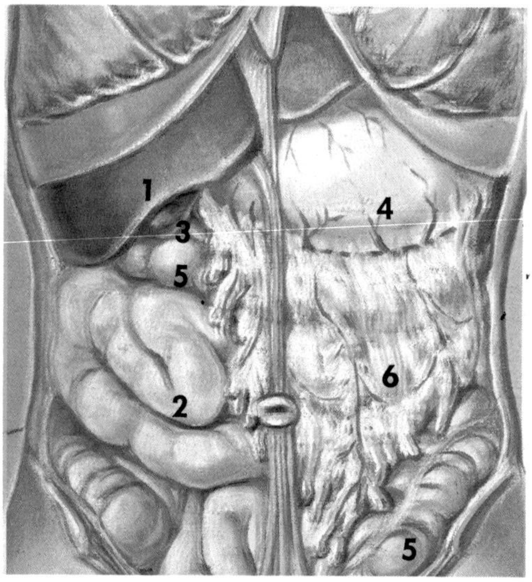

© Denoyer-Geppert Co.

1—LIVER
2—SMALL INTESTINE
3—GALL BLADDER
4—STOMACH
5—LARGE INTESTINE
6—PERITONEUM

There is no real separation between upper and lower (pelvic) abdomen except by an imaginary line which passes through the most prominent part of the sacral bone.

This cavity contains most of the digestive, excretory, and reproductive organs. Most of these organs are covered by a membrane called the *peritoneum.* G. A. D.

SEE ALSO: ANATOMY

Aberration of light see Stars

Abiogenesis see Spontaneous generation

A-Bomb see Bomb

Abortion (uh-BOHR-shun) In human reproduction, abortion is the termination of a fetus before it is born. A spontaneous (unplanned) abortion is often called a "miscarriage." Elective (planned) abortions can be performed by medical doctors. In a few nations where it is now legal, an early PREGNANCY can be ended by taking a pill.

Up to half of all pregnancies end in spontaneous abortions. If this occurs during the first few weeks of a nine-month human pregnancy, a woman may not be aware of it.

Elective abortions are most easily and safely performed during the first twelve weeks of pregnancy. Problems may arise if they are done later. In the 1980s, French scientists developed a drug, RU 486, which, when taken orally, can end early pregnancies. Despite medical advances, elective abortions remain controversial. J.H.

SEE ALSO: BIRTH CONTROL, EMBRYOLOGY, FETUS, PREGNANCY, REPRODUCTIVE SYSTEMS

Abrasives Abrasives are hard solids that rub or wear away other solids by FRICTION. Their action shapes, grinds, and polishes metal, wood, and leather. In nature, windblown dust and waterborne rock abrade other rocks.

A suitable abrasive must be of proper size and must have correct physical properties. It must be harder and of higher melting point than the material being treated.

Natural abrasives most commonly used by man are QUARTZ, SAND, diatomite, tripoli, emery, pumice, and DIAMONDS. Synthetic ones are aluminum oxides, carborundum (silicon carbide), and boron carbide. V. B. I.

Abscess see Infection

Abscission layer see Leaves

Absolute humidity see Humidity

Absolute zero Absolute zero is the coldest that anything can be. Special freezing machines are needed to remove enough heat from a material to bring it almost to absolute zero. A temperature of absolute zero has never actually been reached.

Absolute zero is −459.69° Fahrenheit or −273.16° Centigrade or 0° KELVIN. At that temperature the molecules of a material have stopped their motion. All forms of matter, even gases, become solids.

Familiar materials act strangely at very low temperatures. When cooled to nearly −450°F., soft metals such as lead get as hard as steel. A dropped rubber ball will shatter instead of bounce. Oxygen freezes to a white solid and becomes magnetic like iron. Normally liquid MERCURY looks and acts like hard silver. Even the lightest of gases, hydrogen, becomes liquid at −252.7° C. At −268° C. (+4° Kelvin), HELIUM becomes a liquid and it creeps weirdly up the sides of its container. D. A. B.

SEE ALSO: HEAT, MOLECULAR THEORY, TEMPERATURE SCALES

TEMPERATURE SCALES	WATER BOILS	WATER FREEZES	ABSOLUTE ZERO
CENTIGRADE SCALE	100°	0°	-273.16°
FAHRENHEIT SCALE	212°	32°	-459.69°
KELVIN SCALE	373°	273°	0°

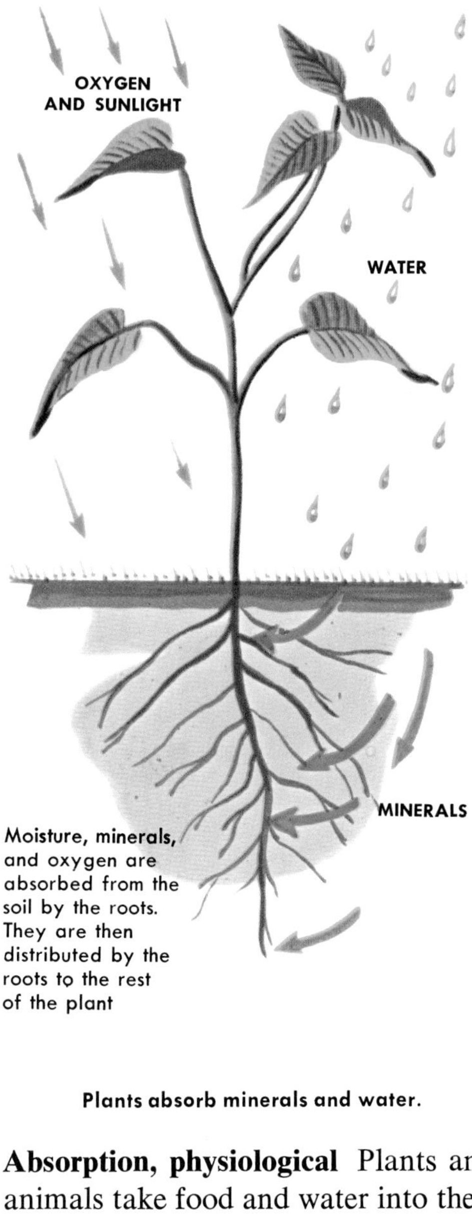
OXYGEN
AND SUNLIGHT
WATER
MINERALS
Moisture, minerals, and oxygen are absorbed from the soil by the roots. They are then distributed by the roots to the rest of the plant

Plants absorb minerals and water.

Absorption, physiological Plants and animals take food and water into their cells by a process called absorption. Medicines or even poisons can also enter the cells in this way. Each cell has a membrane which allows certain substances to pass through it but does not allow other substances to cross it.

One-celled plants and animals can absorb their food directly through the cell membrane. The roots of higher plants absorb water, oxygen, and minerals from the soil through special root hair cells. These nutrients are then distributed throughout the plant by the XYLEM.

The stomach and intestinal cells of higher animals absorb water, salts, SUGARS, FATS, AMINO ACIDS, and VITAMINS from the *alimentary canal.* The blood vessels receive these nutrients and carry them to all parts of the body. The cells of the kidney are able to *reabsorb* water, salts, and sugar that pass through the filter of the glomerulus so that the body can conserve these necessary substances before the elimination of the URINE.

Sometimes absorption can be explained by simple *physical diffusion* through the cell membrane. In many cases, however, absorption is selective and requires the energy supplied by metabolism to provide a *chemical* reaction that makes it possible for certain molecules to pass across the cell membrane. B. B. G.

SEE ALSO: DIFFUSION, METABOLISM, OSMOSIS, ROOT

Absorption of light If a part of a beam of LIGHT passing through something does not come through to the other side, that part has been absorbed. A whole beam of light looks white. Part of a beam appears as a colored light. If white light passes through a piece of colored glass or a colored liquid, the color of the light changes. All the light striking a mirror is not reflected. Part of it is absorbed and changes into heat. If the surface doing the reflecting is dull and dark, then it absorbs more light and reflects less.

White light is a mixture of all colors. When white light strikes a black object all colors are absorbed. When the light strikes a white object all colors are reflected. When white light strikes a colored object, such as a green car, a compromise between white and black occurs. The green car will absorb most colors but not green. This color is reflected giving the car its color.

When white light passes through a colored-transparent surface, such as red glass, a single color is obtained. The glass absorbs most colors. Only the red light gets through. A colored object either reflects its own color or lets only its own color to pass through. All other colors are absorbed.

When a solid is heated until it emits light, this light contains all visible colors. When the light passes through a prism the colors separate to form a *continuous* spectrum. The instrument that uses a prism to study light is a SPECTROSCOPE or spectrometer. When electricity is passed through a container with a small amount of gas or vapor in it, light is emitted. Examination of this light with a spectroscope shows a series of different colored lines. This is an *emission* spectrum. When the light from a heated source passes through the same container, a continuous spectrum with black lines occurs. This is an *absorption* spectrum. The black lines occur where the colored lines occurred in the emission spectrum. A. J. H.

SEE ALSO: LIGHT, SPECTROSCOPE, SPECTRUM

✳ THINGS TO DO

DO BLACK OBJECTS ABSORB MORE LIGHT THAN LIGHT-COLORED OBJECTS?

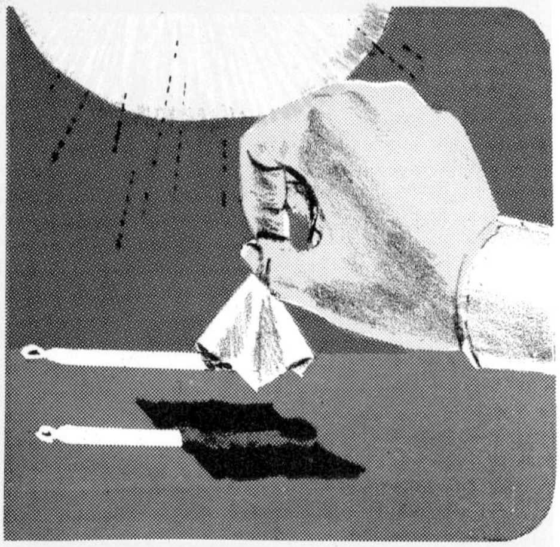

1. **Cover a weather thermometer with a black cloth.**
2. **Cover a second thermometer with a white cloth.**
3. **Set both thermometers in the sun for one-half hour.**
4. **Which thermometer registers a higher degree of temperature? Does the black or white cloth absorb more light and therefore more heat?**

Absorption of sound see Acoustics, Sound

AC (alternating current) see Electricity, Generator

Acceleration (ak-sell-er-A-shun) Acceleration is the rate at which the velocity of an object changes. As a runner starts to sprint toward the end of his run, his speed accelerates. When an airplane starts taxiing down the runway and the passengers are jolted backward in their seats, the speed of the plane is accelerating. Acceleration may be variable as in the case of a rocket after take off or fairly steady as in the case of a freely falling body. It may be negative as in the case of a car whose driver suddenly steps on the brakes.

The speed of an object is the rate at which it moves. Speed is determined by dividing the distance an object moves by the time it takes to move that distance.

$$\text{speed} = \frac{\text{distance}}{\text{time}}$$

The velocity of an object depends on more than distance and time. Velocity depends on direction and the path along which the object moves. The path must be straight. A change in an object's speed implies only a change in its rate of motion. A change in velocity could be a change in the object's rate of motion, direction, or both.

Acceleration of an object is the amount its velocity changes in a given amount of time.

$$\text{acceleration} = \frac{\text{change in velocity}}{\text{time}}$$

Legend holds that Galileo (1564-1642) proved that falling objects have the same acceleration by dropping a bullet and a cannonball from the Leaning Tower of Pisa. Actually, Galileo's experiments were done with inclined planes. His results disproved Aristotle's idea that heavier objects fall faster than lighter ones.

The International Committee on Weights and Measures has set acceleration for the freely falling body at 980.665 cm/sec^2. The acceleration of a falling object depends on height and latitude. The acceleration of a falling body at the equator is 978.039 cm/sec^2. At the poles the figure is 983.217 cm/sec^2. A useful formula relating the distance *(s)* an object falls in time *(t)* is $s = \frac{1}{2}at^2$.

A. J. H. / I. K. F.

SEE ALSO: ARISTOTLE, GALILEO, VELOCITY

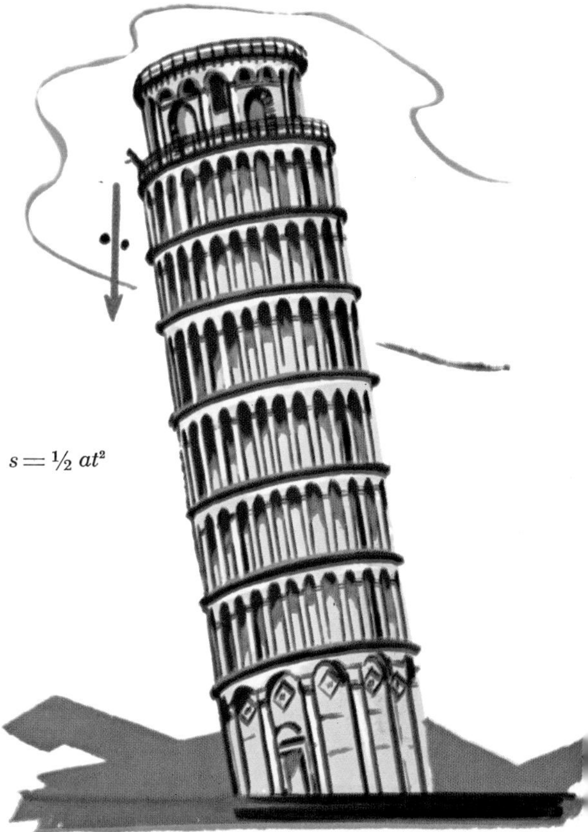

Galileo conducted early experiments in velocity and acceleration

Accelerator The accelerator regulates the speed of an AUTOMOBILE. It opens and closes the throttle valve, letting the fuel-air mixture flow from the CARBURETOR into the cylinders.

Accelerators (particle) Nuclear particle accelerators are machines that give high ENERGY to electrically charged particles and then guide the particles to its targets.

Rays from these targets are detected by delicate sensing and recording devices. The study of these records is part of NUCLEAR SCIENCE.

Nuclear particles include ELECTRONS, PROTONS, DEUTERONS, HELIUM NUCLEI (or ALPHA RAYS) and NEUTRONS.

Argonne National Laboratory Photograph

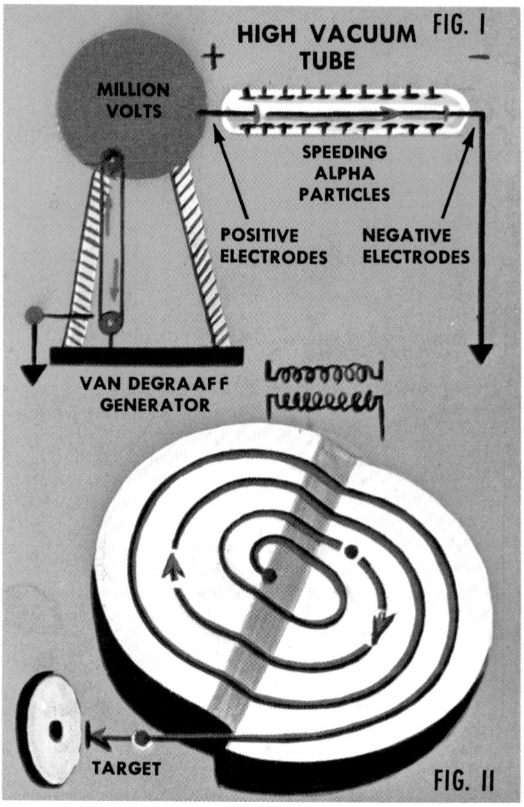

Fig. 1—In the Van de Graaff generator, charged particles are released from a battery along a belt into the sphere. The difference in voltage between the sphere and vacuum tube accelerates the particles. Then they bombard a taraet for useful work

Fig. 2—The cyclotron (as in photo) is made of two D-shaped sections called "dees." The dees have different electrical potentials. The difference makes the particles oscillate up and down increasing their speed near the edge of the dees, where they are ejected onto a target

Accelerators include the *betatron, bevatron, cyclotron, linear accelerator, synchrotron* and *Van de Graaff.*

Each of the several classes of accelerators has theoretical and mechanical features which impose practical upper limits upon the amounts of energy which the machines can impart to particles. Scientists and engineers seek new theories and design improvements which will permit the building of new machines to accomplish more than has been possible with earlier models. Each new machine offers some advantages over former designs, but even so, older types are still useful in many experiments.

There are three main types of accelerators. One is known as an *electrostatic* accelerator, of which the Van de Graaff machine is an example. Also, there are *linear* accelerators and *circular* accelerators. They differ in construction and in the theory upon which they give energy to the particles being accelerated. Each imparts an accelerating force to an electrically charged atomic particle by means of electrical or electromagnetic fields which repel or attract, sometimes alternately, the particle and so cause it to speed up.

The Van de Graaff accelerator is unique in that only a single accelerating impulse is given to each particle. This requires an extremely high voltage difference between the positive and negative poles of the machine. The particle is accelerated continuously during its passage from one end of the machine to the other.

Linear accelerators exert their accelerating influence upon particles which move in relatively straight lines through a series of straight tubes called "drift tubes." Between each two adjacent tubes the electromagnetic fields act upon the particle, much as a ball on a rope might be struck in turn by a number of players at different positions. The length and number of individual tubes are factors in determining the final energy of the particle.

In *circular* accelerators, of which the cyclotron is an example, the magnets are designed and arranged to cause the accelerating particles to move in circular paths. The electromagnets are built in halves, and the particles receive impulses or "kicks" as they move between the two halves. Thus, two such impulses are given to each particle during one trip around the machine. The impulses must be regulated very precisely so that exactly the required impulse is provided to keep the particle moving within the high-vacuum path built into the machine, in spite of the constantly increasing VELOCITY and MASS. R. C. S.

SEE ALSO: NUCLEAR REACTORS

Acceptor atom see Electron borrowing, Electron sharing

Acclimatization (uh-KLY-muh-tuh-ZAY-shun) Acclimatization is the process by which plants and animals adjust to unfamiliar surroundings in order to survive. They acclimate to new conditions in food, temperature, moisture and altitude.

SEE: ADAPTATION, BALANCE OF NATURE

Accommodation Accommodation is the adjustment which the EYE automatically makes in order to see objects at different distances.

SEE ALSO: EYE

Acetabulum see Skeleton

Acetate see Acetic acid, Synthetic fabrics

Acetic acid Acetic acid is a compound. It is a colorless, bitter liquid. Vinegar contains a weak (about 5%) solution of acetic acid. One method of obtaining acetic acid is by distilling wood. Fermentation of fruit juices is the most common commercial process for producing it.

Acetic acid is one of the most common organic acids and one of the most valuable commercially. It will combine with water, alcohol or ether in any proportions. It is an excellent SOLVENT. It is used chiefly in the manufacture of cellulose acetate film and acetate plastics, ester solvents, white lead, Paris green, ASPIRIN and various drugs.

The pure acid is known as "glacial acetic acid" because of the ice-like appearance of the CRYSTALS. Its chemical formula is CH_3COOH. W. J. K.

SEE ALSO: INSECTICIDES, PIGMENT

Acetone (ASS-ah-tone) Acetone is a colorless, flammable, fragrant liquid. Its boiling point is 56.2°C (133.2°F). Acetone is important as a solvent, as in varnishes and plastics. It is also used in the preparation of chloroform, dyestuffs, celluloid photographic films, and many complex organic molecules.

Acetone is more correctly named 2-propanone with the formula CH_3COCH_3. It is made commercially by the controlled oxidation of 2-propanol ($CH_3CH(OH)CH_3$). Acetone dissolves 400 times its own volume of acetylene. Thus it is important in the storage of acetylene. Acetone is found in the human body and can reach high concentrations in persons with diabetes. A. J. H.

SEE ALSO: SOLVENT

Airco Welding Products

Acetylene (uh-SET-uh-leen) Acetylene is a colorless, very explosive gas. When a mixture of acetylene and oxygen is burned, the flame is 3500°C (6332°F). This flame can melt most metals. Acetylene is used in welding and cutting metals.

Acetylene is so explosive it must be dissolved in acetone to store and transport it safely. Acetylene is a very cheap starting material in the commercial synthesis of other organic compounds, such as Orlon, a synthetic fiber; vinyl resins; common plastics; and neoprene, synthetic rubber.

Acetylene is prepared in billion kilogram quantities by the reaction of water and calcium carbide and the combining of molecules of methane. A. J. H.

Acetylsalicylic acid see Aspirin

Achilles, tendon of see Fibrous tissue

Achromatic lens see Lens, man-made

Acid rain see Air pollution

THINGS TO DO

WHICH OF THE FOLLOWING ITEMS ARE ACID? BASIC? NEUTRAL?

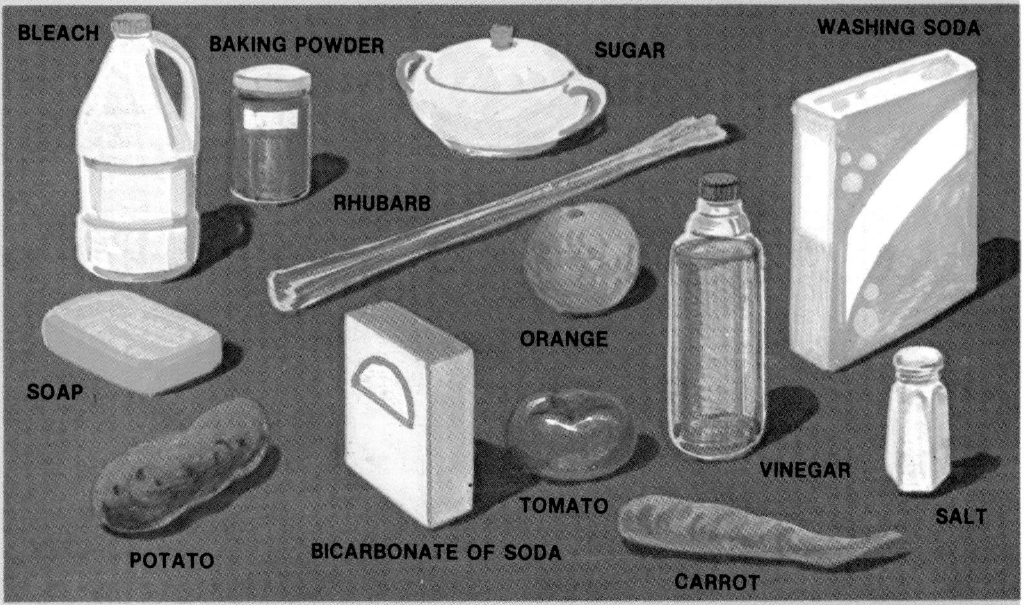

1 Litmus paper is used to determine the acidity and the alkalinity of a material.

2 Acids will turn blue litmus paper pink. Bases will change pink litmus paper to blue. Neutral substances do not affect either color.

3 Use strips of both colors of paper on each of the materials above. The material must be wet or in solution.

Acids and bases Acids are chemicals found in weak form in many foods. Vinegar and most fruits are sour tasting because of their acids. Only grown-up or trained people should work with the stronger acids because they are dangerous to the body.

Both the sourness and also the chemical actions of acids make them useful. When milk or fruit juices stand in a warm place for several days, the bacteria in them will produce acids. This is one step in *fermentation*. This is why many spoiled foods taste sour; but it is also why some good kinds of cheese have a mildly sour flavor.

One very abundant weak acid is not understood as widely as it should be. This is *carbonic acid,* which can be made by forcing carbon dioxide gas into water. Then the solution is bottled. When flavors and sugar are added to the carbonic acid, a carbonated drink—or "soda"—is the result. To increase the flavor of the soft drink, the manufacturers often add other weak acids taken from fruits. They may dissolve white crystals of citric acid or powdered tartaric acid in the soft drink.

The action of the acids formed by foods in our mouths causes our teeth to decay. One common experiment to show the action of acids is to allow a bone or tooth to stand overnight in a glass of lemon juice or vinegar. Afterward the bone or tooth will become soft or pitted with holes. Even the sugar or starch (CARBOHYDRATES) in the candy and cake we eat can be changed to acids overnight. Bacteria act on the bits of these carbohydrates caught between our teeth and ferment them to acids.

In the stomachs of healthy animals and man, weak (1%) HYDROCHLORIC ACID is made by the stomach glands. This dilute stomach acid is needed to start digestion.

BASES (ALSO CALLED ALKALIES)

Bases (alkalies) are the chemical opposites of acids. Solutions of bases turn litmus test paper to blue but acids turn litmus to pink. Bases, like acids, are dangerous to handle because they can cause caustic injury when they touch our bodies.

If equal amounts of an acid and an alkali are mixed in water, a new chemical—a *salt* —is formed. Chemists say that the acid *neutralizes* the base.

Bases are chemicals that always contain *hydroxyl ions* and some metal or metal-like atom. Each hydroxyl ion is composed of one oxygen atom linked to one hydrogen atom. For example, each molecule of the strong base caustic soda or household lye is made up of one atom of the metal sodium-ion and one hydroxyl ion. Thus, lye has the chemical name, sodium hydroxide.

When dry, solid acids and dry alkalies are mixed, no neutralizing chemical change occurs. Ordinary baking powder (*not* baking soda) is such a mixture of dry acid and dry alkaline salt. But when baking powder is mixed with water or milk, a chemical change occurs causing carbon dioxide bubbles to form. The adding of liquid to the dry powder starts the change. So, too, when you add water to a cake mix (containing baking powder), a similar chemical reaction frees CO_2 gas and thus *leavens* the cake batter as it bakes.

AMPHOTERISM

OTHER ACID-ALKALI REACTIONS

Some bases can act both as acids and also as alkalies. For example, zinc hydroxide (a base) in a water solution will act with the stronger base, sodium hydroxide to form the salt sodium zincate (Na_2ZnO_2). In this chemical action, the zinc hydroxide acts as an acid. But when powerful sulfuric acid is added to zinc hydroxide, it acts as bases regularly act. That is, it neutralizes the acid and forms the salt, zinc sulfate ($ZnSO_4$). This ability of a chemical to act as either an acid or a base is called *amphoterism.* Zinc hydroxide is one of several amphoteric chemical compounds.

Soaps are weak bases made from the reacting of fats (or oils) with a strong alkali—usually lye. Household AMMONIA is ammonium hydroxide, a dilute (3%) solution of ammonia gas in water. Ammonia, a base, is used in cleaning and in making other chemicals such as soil salts to fertilize soils. Dry ammonia and some ammonium salts are explosive.

In contrast with bases and their hydroxyl ions, all acids have hydrogen in their molecules in a special form. When acid is put into water, the hydrogen pulls free of the rest of the acid molecule, taking on a positive electrical charge. It is called a *hydrogen ion.* In a water solution these hydrogen ions of an acid give us the distinctive sour taste and account for other chemical properties of acids. The other part of the original acid molecule released during the reaction has a negative charge. Therefore, acids will conduct an electric current when the two live wires from a dry cell open-circuit are plunged into a solution. Hydrogen gas will form at the negative wire. Similarly, bases will conduct electric currents, since their hydroxyl ions are negatively charged and the metallic ion of the base is positively charged. It takes both positive and negative ions for a current to be conducted through a solution.

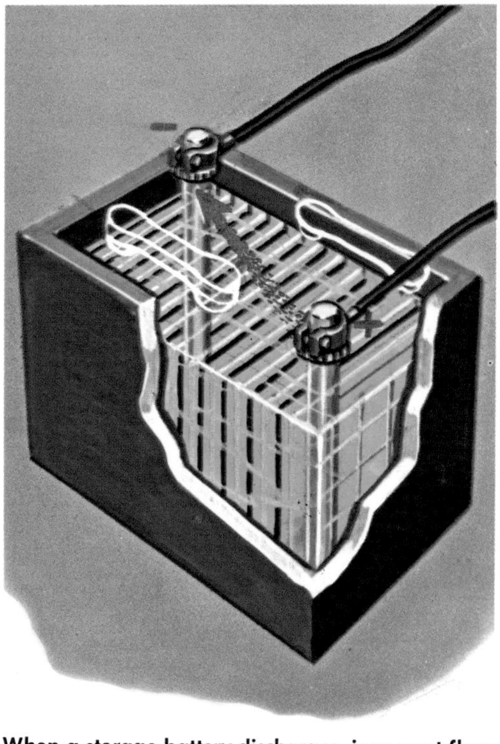

When a storage battery discharges, ions must flow in the electrolyte to replace those lost in chemical reactions at the poles.

Acids (as well as bases) are useful industrially. The storage battery of an automobile, for example, uses sulfuric acid in the water surrounding the cell plates.

Other uses for acids include: removing rust from metals, cleaning stone buildings, neutralizing over-alkaline soils, and making thousands of industrial chemicals. Important organic acids are the amino acids—the building blocks of proteins—and the medicine ASPIRIN (acetylsalicylic acid). Four important commercial acids are sulfuric acid (H_2SO_4), hydrochloric acid (HCl), nitric acid (HNO_3) and acetic acid ($CH_3 \cdot COOH$), found in vinegar. Important bases are sodium hydroxide ($NaOH$)—also called *caustic soda,* potassium hydroxide (KOH) and ammonium hydroxide (NH_4OH). D. A. B.

SEE ALSO: ACETIC ACID, AMINO ACID, CHEMISTRY

Acne (ACK-nee) Acne is a disease. It is not dangerous, nor is it contagious. The pimples, bumps, blackheads, and whiteheads that are often seen on the face are called *acne.* It may also appear on the back, the neck, and the upper chest. Some cases may be very mild while others may become severe. Adults may have acne, but it seems to occur most often between the ages of 13 and 20. Cleanliness plays a large part in preventing complications of *acne.*

At the beginning of PUBERTY, the body makes many changes. The ENDOCRINE GLANDS produce an abundance of hormones. These hormones can stimulate the sebaceous glands in the skin and cause over-secretion. The over-secretion and over-production of cells with subsequent plugging is the primary cause of acne. BACTERIA are often trapped in the pore openings. The bacteria multiply and cause INFLAMMATION, forming pus-filled eruptions and cysts.

Diet no longer seems to play an important role in the control of acne. The skin should be washed no more than three times a day with a mild "superfatted" soap. Topical peeling lotions can be applied to the skin to reduce cyst formation. Serious acne can be treated by a physician with oral antibiotics, topical antibiotic salves, or strong topical peeling agents. Occasionally oral hormones and micro surgery (with injections into the cysts) are used to treat acne. E. S. S.

SEE ALSO: BACTERIA, ENDOCRINE GLANDS, PUBERTY

Acorn see Nuts, Oak

Acorn worm see Platyhelminthes

An acoustic mine is detonated by sound waves

Acoustic weapons Acoustic weapons are devices that are controlled by SOUND. They are usually part of naval warfare, such as homing torpedoes and explosive mines. The *active* WEAPONS send out sounds to locate the target. The *passive* ones locate the destination or are set off by sounds made by the target itself.

SEE: DEPTH SOUNDING, SONAR

Acoustics (uh-KOO-stix) Acoustics is that branch of science which deals with the production, behavior, and reception of sound. In common practice acoustics deals chiefly with the design and control of sound within a limited and confined area, such as a room.

When the source of a sound has ceased, in most rooms the effect of the sound will continue. This is the result of sound waves bouncing back and forth in a closed space. Such a lingering sound is called a *reverberation.* For singing and orchestral design the

✳ **THINGS TO DO**

WHICH IS THE NOISIEST BOX?

Materials: coffee can, cigar box, shoe box lined with corrugated cardboard

1 **Put several stones or marbles in each container.**

2 **Cover tightly. Shake vigorously.**

3 **Which makes the loudest sounds?**

4 **Man uses certain materials in the design and construction of buildings to reduce the intensity of sound vibrations.**

reverberation time should be about two and one-half seconds. A lecture hall functions best when the reverberation time is close to one second. Careful planning and engineering will, in general, make an auditorium usable for both music and speech.

Sounds may reflect off curved interior surfaces in such a way that in some areas the sound will be louder than desirable and in other areas barely audible. Classrooms, libraries, hospitals, and other establishments need to be designed so that noise will be at a minimum. If ceilings, walls, and floors of a room are covered with sound-absorbing surfaces, noise levels are considerably lowered.

The formula is $t = 0.05 \frac{V}{A}$, where t is the time in seconds for the sound to diminish to one-millionth of its initial value, V is the volume in cubic feet of the room and A is the total absorbing power of the room. This formula offers a simple means of determining in advance the acoustics of any room. The formula is the development of W. C. Sabine (1868–1919) and the unit of absorbing power is named after him—sabins. For any room A can be computed. What is needed is the surface area of each material and its acoustic absorption coefficient. Tables of acoustic absorption coefficients are published for most known construction materials. I. K. F.

SEE ALSO: ECHO, SOUND

Acquired characteristics see Lamarck, Jean Baptiste Pierre

Acquired Immune Deficiency Syndrome (AIDS) Aids is a potentially fatal disease that cripples the immune system, the part of the body responsible for fighting illness. People with AIDS die from diseases and cancers the body can no longer fight off. At present, there is no cure or vaccine for AIDS.

AIDS is caused by a virus called the human immunodeficiency virus, or HIV. The virus attacks body cells called helper T cells. These cells function as part of the immune system, which defends the body against outside disease-causing organisms such as bacteria. When helper T cells are destroyed by the HIV virus, the body becomes vulnerable to many kinds of rare infections called opportune infections. AIDS victims are attacked by rare types of cancer, by pneumonia, and by diseases of the skin, lungs, nerves, and brain.

AIDS is a VENEREAL DISEASE. It can be passed from one person to another by sexual contact. It is also transmitted by infected blood or other body fluids. An infected mother can pass the HIV virus to her unborn child. Persons considered most at risk for AIDS are homosexuals and bisexuals, men or women who have sexual contact with many different partners, and drug addicts who share unsterilized hypodermic needles. There is no evidence that AIDS can be transmitted by casual contact such as shaking hands or sharing dishes or bed linens. The virus does not travel through the air like flu germs, and it is not spread by mosquitoes.

A person infected with the HIV virus may not show disease symptoms for years. Once AIDS develops, the patient usually lives for one to two years. At present there is no cure or vaccine for AIDS. In some cases there is evidence that the drug AZT may delay the onset of symptoms, but a cure for AIDS is not expected in the near future.

The best protection a person has against AIDS is prevention. This means that sexually active persons should use condoms, and no one should ever use a hypodermic needle that has been used by someone else.

SEE ALSO: BLOOD, VENEREAL DISEASE

Acquired immunity see Immunity

Acrilan see Synthetic fabrics

Acromegaly (ack-ro-MEG-uh-lee) Acromegaly is a condition which develops in adult life. It is a disturbance of growth in which the bones of the head, face, hands, feet and chest become very large. The jaw protrudes forward and the hands become broad and spadelike.

Acromegaly develops in adults when the front part of the PITUITARY gland produces too much growth hormone. When this happens in children it produces giantism. Sometimes this is caused by a tumor of the pituitary which can be removed by surgery or shrunk by X-ray treatment. Crymotherapy has been used. B. M. H.

ACTH see Cortisone

Actinide elements (ACT-ih-nyde) The actinide series is the group of ELEMENTS with atomic number 89 to 103. It includes ACTINIUM, THORIUM, PROTACTINIUM, URANIUM and the transuranium elements. These elements are similar to each other in their chemical properties and similar to the elements in the lanthanide, or RARE EARTH, series.

SEE: MENDELEEV'S PERIODIC TABLE

Actinium (ak-TIN-i-um) Actinium is a very rare, radioactive element. This colorless, metallic element is found in uranium ores and results from the breakdown of PROTACTINIUM. Andre Debierne discovered actinium in 1899.

Actinium's chemical symbol is Ac. Two isotopes of actinium are found in nature. The isotopes Ac^{228} and Ac^{227} are found in the radioactive decay process of thorium-232 and uranium-235 respectively. There are at least eleven other artificially prepared isotopes. Only Ac^{227}, with a half life of 21.6 years, can be gathered for chemical study.

Actinium's atomic number is 89. Its mass number is 227, and it has a half life of 21.7 years. A. J. H. /D. L. D.

SEE ALSO: RADIOACTIVITY

Adam's apple see Larynx

Adaptation Adaptation is the power of living things to change themselves in order to find food, protect themselves, and bear their young.

Many animals have protective adaptations which keep them safe from their enemies. These protections vary according to the place where the animals live (ENVIRONMENT), and the needs of each kind of animal.

The *coloring* of an animal serves as protection from enemies. For example, white Arctic rabbits and polar bears cannot be seen against the snow. Some

William H. Sonntag

W. H. Sonntag

Jim Brooks

Examples of adaptation include the migration of geese to avoid cold weather; the hard shell of a turtle to protect its soft body; and the coloring of a polar bear, which helps it blend with the snow.

Photos courtesy National Fish & Wildlife Service

animals change color with the seasons and therefore have a means of hiding from their enemies. Other animals copy their environment. A walking stick hides by looking like the twigs of trees. The turtle's shell protects its soft body.

Adaptation may involve the *behavior* of living things as well as body structure. Not all birds adjust to changing seasons. Instead, they *migrate* to a mild climate in late summer or early autumn. Some insects, such as certain butterflies, also migrate. Some animals, such as ground squirrels, store up excessive fat and become inactive in winter. This is known as HIBERNATION. Community living is another adaptation for survival. ANTS and BEES have a very highly developed form of community living.

Animals adapt according to their needs for obtaining food, water and oxygen. This may involve body structure, behavior, or a combination of these. The thickness of the skin of many kinds of animals prevents evaporation of moisture. The water spider spins a bell-shaped web and fills it with air from bubbles which collect on the spider's legs.

Man is one of the most adaptive of living things. Some human adaptations are evolutionary or hereditary. Others are individual and are not passed on to succeeding generations. The body of man, as well as other animals, is able to build up immunities to foreign substances. Man's use of clothing, food, and shelter are also examples of adaptation.

SEE ALSO: EVOLUTION, PROTECTIVE COLORATION

Adder see Snakes

Adder's tongue fern see Wild flowers

Addiction Addiction is a condition in which a person has a physical need as well as a psychological dependency for certain things, such as NARCOTICS or liquor.

Withdrawing narcotics, such as morphine or heroin, from a person who is addicted can cause severe changes in his or her physical well-being, resulting in sweating, vomiting, and even convulsions. When liquor is withdrawn from a person addicted to alcohol, he or she can go into delirium tremens, commonly known as "DT's." Alcohol addiction is often responsible for many automobile accidents and days lost from jobs. Illegal narcotics addiction contributes greatly to crimes for money. Cigarette smoking, while a bad *habit* and dangerous to health, is not a true addiction.
E.S.S.

Adding machine An adding machine is a COMPUTER that carries out addition and subtraction mechanically. The numbers on the keyboard control wheels inside the machine. As the numbers are punched, the machine records the answer. Some adding machines can also be used for multiplication and division. Today, much of the work once done by adding machines is done by hand calculators or other small computers.

Most calculators use electronic circuits. This has made much faster calculations possible. It has also been possible to reduce the size of the instrument. Some calculators are small enough to fit in a pocket. However, most calculators do not produce a record of each number entered as do the adding machines that use tape.
M. M. L.

Addison's disease The wasting away of the ADRENAL GLANDS will produce Addison's disease. The glands can no longer produce the hormone called CORTISONE.

The entire METABOLISM is disturbed when too little of this hormone is present. The person becomes weak and tired. He may develop a brownish skin tone over the entire body. Blood pressure is very low. The blood loses sodium salt and sugar. The amount of potassium salt increases. There is a wasting away of muscle tissue and weight loss. Digestive trouble and loss of reproductive powers are common. The disease may be produced by tumors, such as cancer, by tuberculosis, or by injury to the adrenals. It is successfully treated by giving cortisone and salt. President John F. Kennedy had Addison's disease.
B. M. H. / E. S. S.

SEE ALSO: ADRENALIN, CORTISONE

Addition see Arithmetic

Adenoids The adenoids are two islands of lymphatic tissue in the back of the passageway leading from the nose to the throat. They vary in size but sometimes in children they grow so large as to obstruct the passage and prevent breathing through the nose. They may then have to be removed by surgery.

The adenoids, like the *tonsils* at the sides of the throat, are helpful in warding off infections of the nose and throat. They may become severely inflamed when infected by *streptococcus,* a condition that may lead to rheumatic fever or kidney disease.
B. M. H.

SEE ALSO: LYMPHATIC SYSTEM

ADF see Direction finder

Adhesion A drop of water on oily paper or on a smooth table top can be seen to round up a little. Another drop on rough paper or wood will flatten out more and stick. But a drop of mercury will round up almost into a half-ball shape on the oily surface or the plain paper or the wood. The mercury has weak adhesion for the paper, compared with the strong *adhesive forces* pulling water to many other materials.

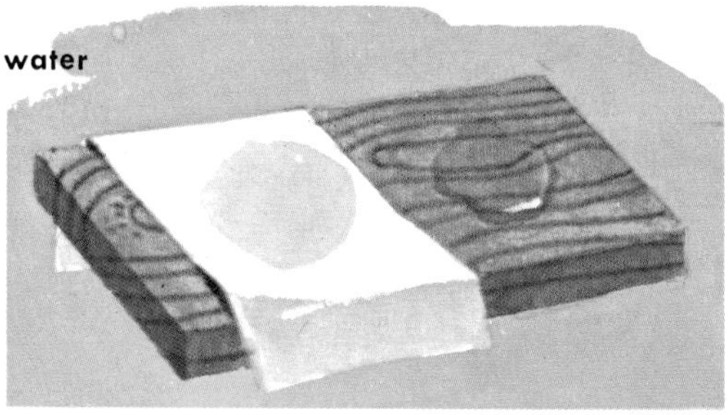

Water adheres to paper and wood.

Scientifically, adhesion is the force between molecules attracting two different kinds of materials. D. A. B.
SEE ALSO: COHESION

Adhesive An adhesive is any chemical that will stick—or bond—two pieces of material together. Glue, library paste, and plastic cements are household adhesives. There are many kinds of industrial adhesives.

Expert adhesive chemists class adhesives by three kinds of action: structural, holding, and sealing (or *calking,* as for boats). Cellophane tape works as a holding adhesive when it fastens an object to a wall; but it acts structurally to join paper. Casein or fish glue binds a heavy object securely if it is held until the joints dry.

A wide range of adhesives is needed to deal with the many problems met when fastening objects together. Cellulose nitrate dries very quickly and is commonly used as a model cement. Polyvinyl resin, or white glue, is often used to repair furniture. Hide glue, or "hot glue," is also used to mend wooden objects. A rubber-based adhesive is used to bond fabric or rubber auto trim. Polyester resin adhesive is used to repair the fiberglass boats or dented auto bodies. Epoxy adhesive is a combination of two liquids and dries with minimal loss of space to form a strong bond. Cyanoacrylates are a new group of strong bonding glues. Contact cement is used on floor tile. A. J. H. /D. A. B.

Adipose tissue see Fat, adipose tissue

Adirondacks see North America

Adobe see Brick

Adolescence (add-uh-LESS-uhns) Adolescence is the period of sexual development and uneven physical growth between PUBERTY and maturity. It usually includes ages 12 to 20. The adolescent may have emotional problems due to his efforts to achieve independence and adjust to the opposite sex.

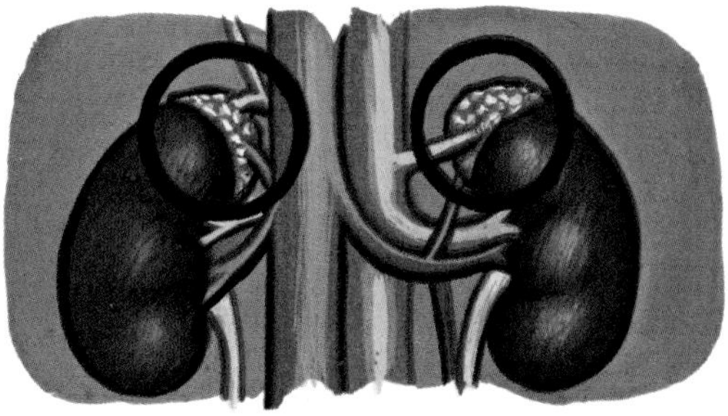

Adrenal glands lie above the kidneys.

Adrenal glands (add-REE-nal) The adrenal glands are two small organs in the body of higher animals. They are just above the kidneys. Although they are small, they are important. Without them the animal dies.

The adrenals are one member of the system of ENDOCRINE GLANDS that have no ducts to the outside. They secrete their chemical HORMONES directly into the blood stream.

The adrenal gland is actually made up of two separate parts, which are formed from two totally different types of cells when the animal first develops. The inner part is called the *medulla* and comes from the same type of cells that form the NERVOUS SYSTEM. The outer part is called the *cortex* and is formed from the kind of cells that also form the KIDNEY and the sex organs. It is not surprising then to find that the hormone produced by the medulla is like the nervous system in its effects. Similarly, the hormones produced by the cortex are related to the kidney and sex organs.

The medulla secretes the hormone ADRENALIN (epinephrine). It is stimulated by the nervous system and has a similar action. Under conditions of stress it marshals all the resources of the body to fight danger.

The adrenal cortex secretes many hormones. CORTISONE, which is one of these hormones, helps the body to recover from a stress after adrenalin has met the first danger. *Aldosterone* is also formed in the adrenal cortex and is a vital hormone. It maintains the proper ratio of sodium to potassium ions in the body tissues. Thus, the amount of body fluid is regulated by this hormone.

Some of the adrenal cortical hormones act in the same way as ESTROGEN, PROGESTERONE, and ANDROGEN which are sex hormones. The adrenal cortical hormones, like the sex hormones, are steroids.

The amount of hormone produced by the adrenal cortex is governed by the PITUITARY GLAND. Oversecretion of the adrenal cortical hormones can cause VIRILISM. Adrenal virilism is a condition in which the oversecretion causes body changes. A young boy or girl, or a woman, may grow hair upon the face, develop a deeper voice and larger muscles, and begin to take on the characteristics of a man in the reproductive parts of the body. Since ANDROGEN (male sex hormone) is part of the adrenal secretion, this increase in androgen causes the masculine effects. B. B. G.

SEE ALSO: ADDISON'S DISEASE, ENDOCRINE GLANDS, REPRODUCTIVE SYSTEM, STEROID

Adrenalin Adrenalin (also called *epinephrine*) is a HORMONE made by the adrenal glands of animals. It helps the body to react quickly to danger.

In normal amounts adrenalin maintains the BLOOD PRESSURE. In case of STRESS, such as injury, fear or anger, the nervous system stimulates the adrenal medulla (the inner core of the adrenal gland) to release large amounts of adrenalin into the blood stream. The heart beats faster, the blood vessels contract, and the blood pressure rises. The bronchial tubes of the lungs expand so that more air can be taken in. Sugar that has been stored in the liver is brought into circulation in the blood for use as fuel. The muscles are prepared for action. B. B. G.

Adsorption Adsorption is the gathering together, or ADHESION, of molecules of solids, liquids or gases in a thin layer on the surface of a solid body.

SEE: CHEMISTRY, GAS

Adventitious see Root

Aeration see Purification of water

Aerial see Antenna (electronic)

Aerobic (ay-uh-ROH-bick) Aerobic refers to the dependence of living things on oxygen. *Aerobic* bacteria grow in air-rich liquids or foods where *anaerobic* bacteria fail to grow.

Leonardo Da Vinci's 1490 flying machine

Aerodynamics (air-oh-dye-NAM-micks) Aerodynamics is the science of air movement around all objects that move and stand still. Aerodynamics explains how airplanes fly. Air movement and its effects are very important to those who design moving vehicles such as airplanes and automobiles, and to the men who plan buildings and bridges.

There are three principles that form the basis of aerodynamics. First, scientists have learned that moving air will push up against flat surfaces held at an angle to the wind; for example, windmills and sailboats. Secondly, the force of air under a moving object pushes it upward. Finally, the surfaces of an object will move toward a rapidly-moving air stream above it.

The lifting force of the airplane wing is produced in two ways. One way is the direct pressure of the air against the tilted wing. Much more important is the lift generated through the effect of Bernoulli's principle. This principle, discovered by the Swiss mathematician, DANIEL BERNOULLI, states that a gas, like air, passing rapidly over a surface exerts less pressure against the surface than a GAS moving more slowly. Aircraft wings are designed to take advantage of this principle by having the top surface curved. Thus, the air moving across the top has farther to travel than that below the wing resulting in a more rapid flow. The air pressure on the top of the wing surface is then *less* than that exerted by the slower moving air across the bottom, thereby creating lift.

Aeronautical engineers must design aircraft so that the *lifting* force of the wings must overcome the force of *gravity*. The forward *thrust* force provided by the propeller or jet engine must also overcome the *drag* force or the resistance of the air to the aircraft movement. Drag is reduced by giving the aircraft a streamlined shape.

A knowledge of aerodynamics is important to designers of buildings and bridges. WIND loads on these structures must be carefully planned before they are erected, so that they offer the least resistance to the winds for greater stability.

Though serious study of aerodynamics began during World Wars I and II when great numbers of airplanes were needed, the theories of air movement date back to LEONARDO DA VINCI in the sixteenth century. From his diagrams of birds in flight, he designed a flying machine and even proposed that man could fly with mechanical bird-like wings.

In the 1880's, Otto Lilienthal experimented with air movement in his glider study, and made the first successful glider flight. Samuel Langley in 1891 published the first scientific papers on aerodynamics, and he even flew an airplane model. In 1903 the WRIGHT BROTHERS were successful in getting a powered airplane to fly.

Much of today's aerodynamic research is devoted to the problems of *supersonic* (faster than sound) and *high-altitude* flight. High-speed flight has created many new problems. Air FRICTION and compression cause heat which weakens metals; great air pressures many times the force of a hurricane are encountered and the air flowing around the aircraft changes its characteristics.

As missiles and space craft are developed, new shapes must be designed to cope with the special problems of re-entering the atmosphere from space.

Research in slow speed flight aerodynamics is also being undertaken to develop aircraft which are able to land, take off and remain airborne at very slow speeds. R. J. J.

SEE ALSO: AERONAUTICS; AIRCRAFT; AIRPLANE; FLIGHT, PRINCIPLES OF

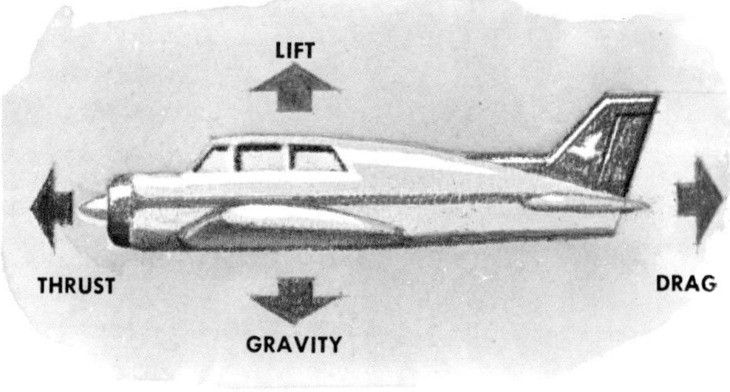

THE FOUR FORCES IN LEVEL FLIGHT

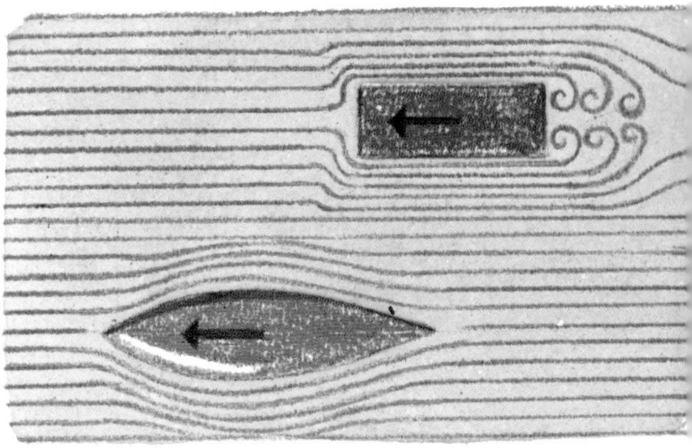
STREAMLINING INCREASES SPEED

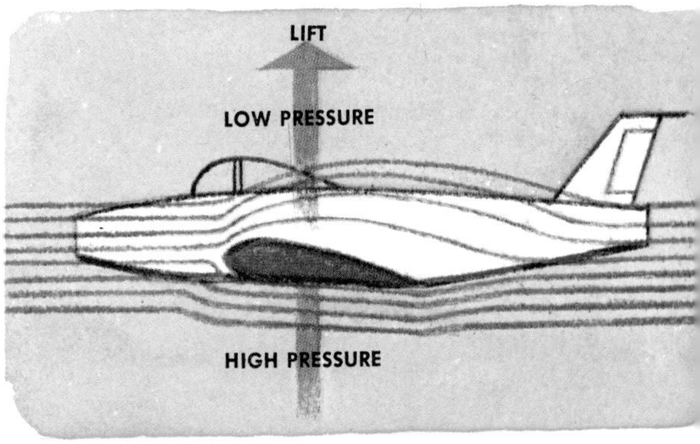

DIFFERENCES IN AIR PRESSURE CREATE LIFT

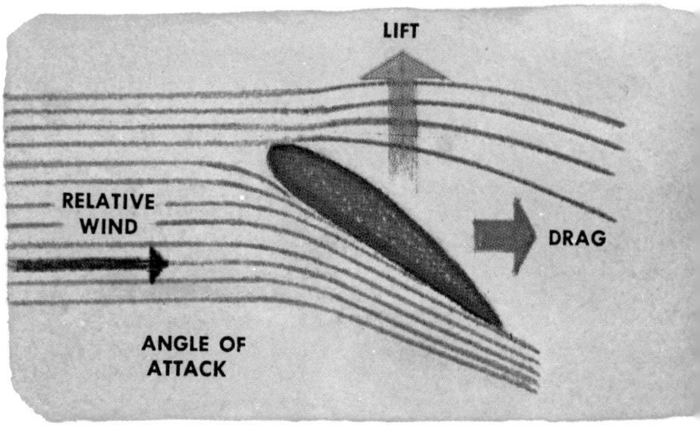

Aeronautics (air-uh-NAWT-ticks) Aeronautics is the art and science of flight through the air. Advances in science have brought aeronautics from the hot air BALLOON flights of 200 years ago to today's supersonic (faster than sound) jet flights of the Lockheed SR-71 "Blackbird" Air Force bomber at a world record 2,086 mph (3,357.09 km/ph) over a closed-circuit course. Aeronautics can be classified into two major fields: lighter-than-air craft and heavier-than-air craft.

LIGHTER-THAN-AIR CRAFT

Lighter-than-air craft were the first successful man-carrying flying vehicles. In 1250, Roger Bacon recorded the idea that an object would float in air in much the same way as an object floats in water. The hot air balloon was the first application of this idea, with later use of light gases such as HYDROGEN.

The control of balloon flight is limited to the dropping of ballast for altitude gain and the release of gas for descent. The more practical airship was developed in 1852 by Henri Giffard who added a steam-engine powered propeller to an elongated balloon. Long-distance flights over specific routes became practical after vertical and horizontal fins were added, along with more powerful engines. These airships became known as dirigibles and zeppelins.

HEAVIER-THAN-AIR CRAFT

A more successful approach to controlled flight has been the heavier-than-air branch of aeronautics. The earliest of these vehicles were gliders, which were simply pushed off of hilltops into flight. They were dependent upon favorable air currents and winds to stay aloft once airborne.

The WRIGHT BROTHERS made the first powered flight in a heavier-than-air craft in 1903. Just four years later, in 1907, the Frenchmen Charles and Gabriel Voisin began the world's first airplane manufacturing company. Commercial airline companies were active in the U.S. and Europe before 1920, although the first long-term U.S.

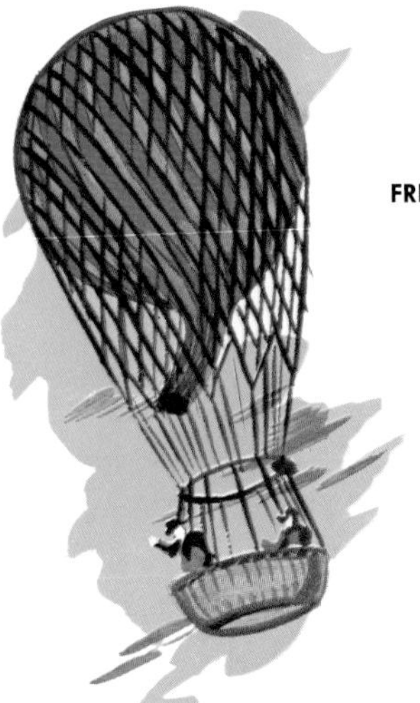

FREE BALLOON

HANG-TYPE LILIENTHAL GLIDER

WRIGHT BROTHERS' AIRCRAFT, 1903

The Boeing Company

Boeing's 747-400, and inside its flight deck

airline company did not begin scheduled service until 1926.

The HELICOPTER, able to take off vertically, and airplanes powered by JET PROPULSION were first flown in 1939. In 1947, U.S.A.F. pilot Charles Yeager flew a Bell X-1 plane faster than the speed of sound. The Concorde jetliner began carrying commercial passengers faster than the speed of sound in 1976. During the late 1970s and the 1980s, experiments were made with lightweight airplanes powered only by human muscles.

Development of modern aircraft has been accelerated by the use of WIND TUNNELS. With these devices, designers can study the effects of varying air speeds without actually flying an aircraft. Often, special dyes are added so that air flowing around all parts of a craft can be seen. AERONAUTICS has also been assisted by the use of COMPUTERS to simulate movement of various designs through air.

MODERN FLIGHT

Early pilots had few controls and instruments. They relied on their eyes and their sense of balance to tell them their position in the air. Today, computers and other electronic devices are being used to assist pilots.

Electronic Flight Information Systems (EFIS) present a wide variety of information on television screens. Developed in the 1980s and 1990s, EFIS collect and display data from airplanes, airports, weather stations, and communication centers in an attempt to make flying safer and more efficient than ever before possible. R.J.J./J.H.

SEE ALSO: AERODYNAMICS; AIRPLANE; FLIGHT, PRINCIPLES OF; INSTRUMENT LANDING SYSTEM; INSTRUMENT PANEL

Aerosol (AIR-ruh-sall) A cloud of tiny particles floating in the air is an aerosol. These particles can be liquid or solid, such as fog or dust. Familiar examples of aerosols are spray cans of paint or deodorant.

The size of the particles is important in an aerosol. Particles are measured in microns (one-millionth of a meter). Aerosols range from .01-100 microns. Fog ranges from 1-50 microns. It is difficult to see the particles if the diameter is less than one micron. From 0.1-1.0 microns, it is called smoke. For example, tobacco smoke ranges from 0.1-1.0 microns.

Aerosols have many sources, such as volcanoes. Salt particles produced by sea spray are another. Plants produce many aerosols, i.e. spores, pollens, and terpenes. Terpenes, plant-produced aerosols, cause the Great Smokey Mountain hazes. Ash from forest fires, industry, and fuel consumption produce great quantities of aerosols.

The largest aerosols are trapped in the nose and throat. Smaller aerosols pass into the lungs where they stay. Aerosols in the lungs can lead to bronchial ASTHMA, emphysema, or CANCER. A. J. H.

SEE ALSO: AIR POLLUTION, OZONE

Aerospace (AIR-oh-spayss) Aerospace is the total expanse upward and outward from the earth's surface and also refers to research, development and production of vehicles and devices for use in the ATMOSPHERE and SPACE.
SEE: AIRCRAFT, AVIATION, MISSILES, ROCKETS, SPACE VEHICLES

Africa Africa is the second-largest continent. It covers 11.7 million square miles (30.3 million square kilometers.) Africa is three times as large as the United States.

Africa is almost as wide as it is long, its width being less by about 300 miles (482.8 kilometers.) Over one-half of Africa is made up of a series of plateaus. Its coastline has few indentations, and for that reason there are few natural harbors to be found. The lack of harbors was one of many reasons that the development of Africa has been slow.

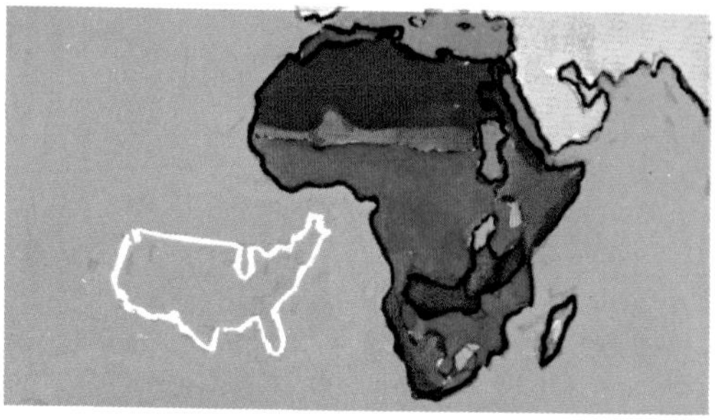

Africa is three times larger than the United States.

The equator divides Africa in two, but there is much more land area north of the equator than south of it because of the great bulge of land toward the Atlantic Ocean.

African climate is extremely variable, especially in the amounts of precipitation received. Some parts of the Sahara Desert receive less than 10 inches (25.4 centimeters) of rainfall per year but other areas of the tropical rain forest receive well over 200 inches (508 centimeters).

LAND FORMS

The coastline of Africa is so smooth that few good harbors are available for seaports.

Africa, the continent most deficient in plains, consists essentially of one great plateau which has, however, several distinctive subdivisions. These include the Sahara, the Congo Basin, and the Ethiopian Highlands. The main plateau of Africa is dissected by a rift valley system. A rift valley is a gigantic fracture (fault) in the earth's crust. It is formed as the crust breaks and slowly sinks down between parallel fractures.

One of the largest lakes of the rift valley system is Lake Victoria. Only Lake Superior is larger as a freshwater lake. Lake Victoria is also the main source of the Nile River.

There are no great mountain systems like

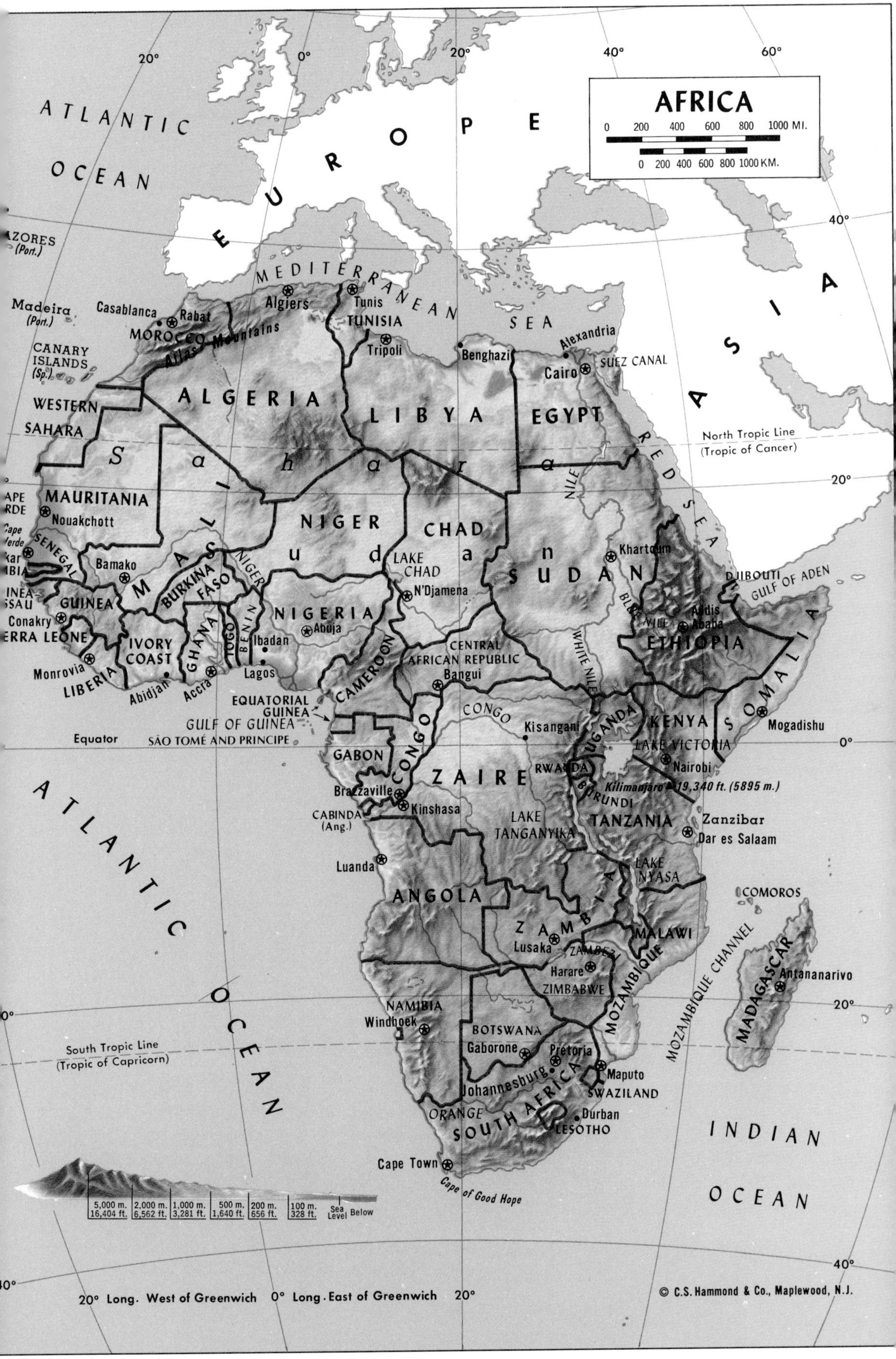
AFRICA
0 200 400 600 800 1000 MI.
0 200 400 600 800 1000 KM.
ATLANTIC OCEAN
EUROPE
ASIA
MEDITERRANEAN SEA
AZORES (Port.)
Madeira (Port.)
CANARY ISLANDS (Sp.)
Casablanca
Rabat
MOROCCO
Atlas Mountains
Algiers
Tunis
TUNISIA
Tripoli
Benghazi
Alexandria
Cairo
SUEZ CANAL
WESTERN SAHARA
ALGERIA
LIBYA
EGYPT
RED SEA
North Tropic Line (Tropic of Cancer)
Sahara
Sudan
NILE
MAURITANIA
Nouakchott
SENEGAL
MALI
Bamako
NIGER
BURKINA FASO
CHAD
LAKE CHAD
N'Djamena
SUDAN
Khartoum
DJIBOUTI
GULF OF ADEN
BLUE NILE
WHITE NILE
Addis Ababa
ETHIOPIA
SOMALIA
Mogadishu
GUINEA
Conakry
SIERRA LEONE
Monrovia
LIBERIA
IVORY COAST
Abidjan
GHANA
Accra
TOGO
BENIN
Ibadan
Lagos
NIGERIA
Abuja
CAMEROON
CENTRAL AFRICAN REPUBLIC
Bangui
EQUATORIAL GUINEA
GULF OF GUINEA
SÃO TOMÉ AND PRINCIPE
Equator
GABON
CONGO
Brazzaville
Kinshasa
CABINDA (Ang.)
ZAIRE
Kisangani
UGANDA
KENYA
LAKE VICTORIA
Nairobi
RWANDA
BURUNDI
Kilimanjaro 19,340 ft. (5895 m.)
TANZANIA
Zanzibar
Dar es Salaam
LAKE TANGANYIKA
LAKE NYASA
Luanda
ANGOLA
ZAMBIA
Lusaka
ZAMBEZI
MALAWI
Harare
ZIMBABWE
MOZAMBIQUE
MOZAMBIQUE CHANNEL
COMOROS
MADAGASCAR
Antananarivo
NAMIBIA
Windhoek
BOTSWANA
Gaborone
Pretoria
Maputo
Johannesburg
SWAZILAND
ORANGE
SOUTH AFRICA
Durban
LESOTHO
Cape Town
Cape of Good Hope
South Tropic Line (Tropic of Capricorn)
INDIAN OCEAN
5,000 m. 16,404 ft.
2,000 m. 6,562 ft.
1,000 m. 3,281 ft.
500 m. 1,640 ft.
200 m. 656 ft.
100 m. 328 ft.
Sea Level
Below
20° Long. West of Greenwich
0° Long. East of Greenwich
© C.S. Hammond & Co., Maplewood, N.J.

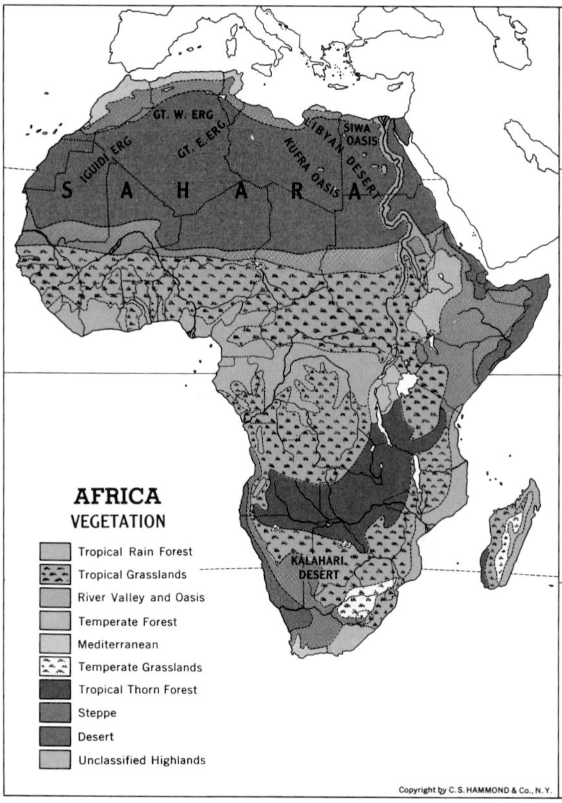

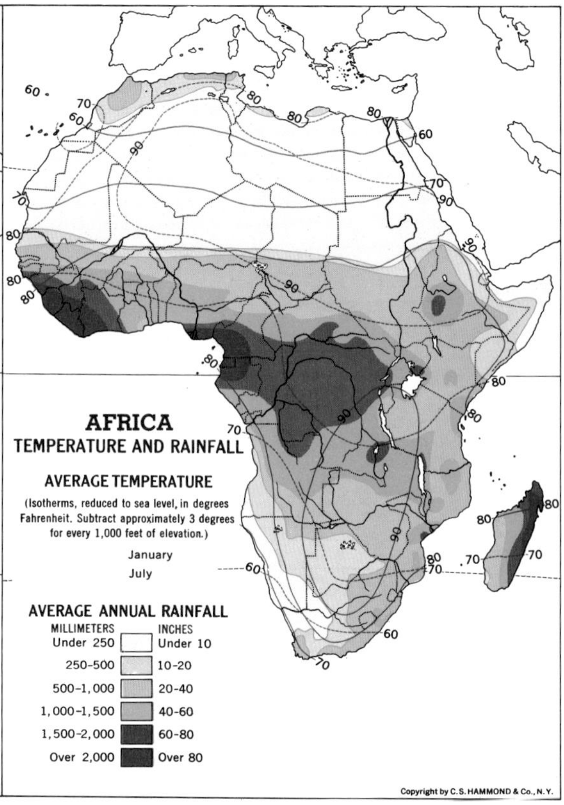

those of North and South America. The largest mountain range is the Atlas Mountains in northwest Africa with an elevation of about 14,000 feet (4267.2 meters). The highest mountain peak in Africa is Mt. Kilimanjaro, which lies among valleys in East Africa. Its height is 19,340 feet (5,895 meters).

CLIMATE

The climate in Africa at the equator is *rainy tropical*. This climate extends from the Guinea Coast on the west through the Congo Basin, with a break in the highlands of East Africa, and a reappearance on the Zanzibar coast in the east. In this area there are no changes in season, and night and day are of equal length. Average rainfall is about 100 inches (254 centimeters) annually, but in the west, the Cameroons may have as much as 400 inches (1016 centimeters) per year. Daytime temperatures average 80-82° F. (26.7-27.8° C.). No extremes of high temperatures are found here, but the weather is oppressive because of the high HUMIDITY.

North and south of the rainy tropic belt across Africa, the amount of rainfall decreases. In these *monsoon tropical* belts, about 500 miles (804.67 kilometers) wide, the wet and dry seasons are very distinct. The plants are mostly grouped trees and grasses. The grasses may reach heights of 10 to 12 feet (3.05 to 3.66 meters). The GIRAFFE is a typical animal of this area.

Beyond the monsoon tropical climate in both directions is the *semi-arid tropical* climate with less rainfall. The semi-arid climate merges into the *arid tropical* climate where true desert conditions prevail. The Sahara in the north and the Kalahari Desert in the south are in this climate.

RIVERS AND DRAINAGE

The *Nile River* rises among snow-capped mountains and large lakes in east central Africa. The rains and melting snows on the mountains reach a peak at the end of the summer, creating flooding on the lower river. For thousands of years the floods deposited silt to renew the soil's fertility for farmers in the Nile Valley. Since the Aswan High Dam was built in the 1960s, the river valley no longer floods.

San Diego Zoo

San Diego Zoo

Christine Hagel

San Diego Zoo

Patrick Cavanaugh

San Diego Zoo

Some well-known African animals include (Top) rhinos, elephants, lions, (Bottom) elands, zebras, and giraffes.

Although the Nile is the second largest river in the world (after the Amazon in SOUTH AMERICA), the *Congo River* in equatorial Africa has a much greater flow of water at its mouth on the Atlantic. Its main source tributaries, the *Laulaba* and the *Chambezi* arise very near the sources of the Nile in east Africa, only a slight elevation separating the beginning of the two great drainage systems. The Congo system is 3000 miles (4828.03 kilometers) from source to mouth.

The *Zambezi River* also rises in east Africa and flows south and east into the Indian Ocean. The great Victoria Falls are on the Zambezi. The Niger River flows north of, and parallel to, the Congo for 2000 miles (3218.69 kilometers) and is the third longest river in Africa.

PLANTS AND ANIMALS

The tropical rain forests of Africa are sometimes called jungles. The rain forest has a high canopy of trees that act as an umbrella over the forest floor. As a result the floor receives little light. Little plant growth is to be found. The amount of plant and animal life, both in number and kind, is tremendous. Most of the animals live in the trees above the forest floor.

Some of the animals that live on the jungle floor, in the streams, or frequently descend from the trees are: gorilla, ape, baboon, antelope, okapi, bush cow, crocodile, hippopotamus, forest pig, and many snakes. The big game animals, such as lions and elephants, are found in the plateau country of east Africa. The birds of the jungle and lake country include the flamingo, peacock, hornbill, and long-tailed sunbird.

Dense rain forests and jungles may be found along the Guinea Coast and the Zaire. The forests contain many trees and valuable woods like MAHOGANY, walnut, and EBONY, and many palms, ferns, and vines.

Africa has a host of exotic flowers, especially in the tropical regions. Many familiar garden flowers originate here, such as gladioli, calla lilies, geraniums, marigolds, tulips, iris and amaryllis.

The insects of Africa include the driver

(or soldier) ant, termite, scorpion, tsetse fly, mosquito, locust, rhinoestrus (botfly) and many varieties of butterflies, moths, and bees.

NATURAL RESOURCES

The continent of Africa has a wealth of mineral resources. Most are mined by large international corporations, giving limited financial help to the people living there. Much of Africa's natural wealth is sent to other parts of the world.

Central and southern Africa is the world's leading producer of diamonds and gold. Much of that wealth is found in the Republic of South Africa, at the southern tip of the continent. Gold was first discovered in the rocks of South Africa's Witwatersrand district in 1865. Johannesburg, in the center of the enormous Witwatersrand goldfield, has been called "the city of gold." Ghana also has large deposits of gold. When it was a British colony, Ghana was known as the Gold Coast. A huge diamond rush began in South Africa when a 21-carat stone was found near Hopetown in 1867. Two years later, the magnificent "Star of South Africa," an 83½-carat diamond, was discovered. Today, South Africa is the leading producer of diamonds in the world. Most are found in a type of rock called kimberlite that once was molten and flowed through formations known as volcanic pipes. Botswana is also an important diamond producer.

Other minerals mined in Africa include cobalt, copper, iron, lead, manganese, uranium, and zinc. The continent has the world's largest known reserves of bauxite (from which aluminum is extracted), chromium, antimony, platinum, and manganese.

Large deposits of PETROLEUM and NATURAL GAS have been discovered in Africa during the second half of the twentieth century. The major petroleum-bearing territories are in the dry areas of northern Africa, including Algeria, Egypt, and Libya, and in off-shore drilling sites around Angola, Gabon, and Nigeria. Africa is not among the leading producers of coal, but some significant deposits are found in South Africa, Zimbabwe, Nigeria, and Zaire.

Because of its many huge lakes and rivers, Africa potentially can create more HYDROELECTRIC POWER than any other continent (about 40 percent of the world's total). Much of that potential (about half) is concentrated in Zaire. Important hydroelectric dams include the Aswan High Dam in Egypt, the Kariba Dam on the Zambezi River, and the Volta Dam in Ghana. P.P.S./J.H.D./J.H.

SEE ALSO: BAUXITE, COAL, DIAMONDS, GOLD, HYDROELECTRIC POWER, JUNGLE, NATURAL GAS, PETROLEUM

African sleeping sickness see Sleeping sickness

African violet (Saintpaulia) see Violet

Afterburner An afterburner is a device used in a turbojet, or "jet," engine to increase the thrust when more power is needed. *Thrust* is the force which pushes the plane forward. The afterburner reheats gases after they leave the TURBINE and before they enter the discharge nozzle.

SEE: FLIGHT, PRINCIPLES OF; JET PROPULSION

Agar see Algae, Bacteriology

Agassiz, Louis (1807-1873) Louis Agassiz was a Swiss naturalist who was an authority on sea animals. He also was keenly interested in the movement of glaciers over Europe, and he gave the world its first real understanding of the moving mountains of ice.

In 1846 Agassiz came to America to lecture at Harvard University, and he remained there for twenty-five years as a professor of natural history. During this time he began collections which later were included in the Harvard Museum.

Because of his deep interest in sea animals, he established a summer school laboratory on an island in Buzzards Bay off the coast of Massachusetts. Here the sea animals could be studied in their natural surroundings.

Professor Agassiz was an avid explorer. He went on expeditions to Brazil and to the waters around Cuba, and he sailed around Cape Horn to California. He was a prolific writer, who left the world a wealth of material on natural science. D. H. J.

Agate (AGG-it) Agate is a waxy form of the mineral QUARTZ. Its colors are arranged in regular bands or distinct patterns. Cut and polished agates are favorite gem stones for rock collectors.

Agates are found throughout the world. India, Brazil, and Uruguay are known for their fine agates. The Lake Superior region of North America is rich in agates.

ONYX is a variety of agate in which the parallel bands are perfectly straight. It is often used for the cutting of cameos. Moss agate is another variety which appears to have a fern-like design in it. P. P. S.

Courtesy Society For Visual Education, Inc.

Agate specimens

Ageratum (ad-juh-RAY-tum) An ageratum is a small plant used for borders or beds in flower gardens. The small flowers are fluffy groups of blue, white, or pink blooms. Each tiny flower is tube shaped.

Ageratum plants grow from 6 to 9 inches (15.24 to 22.86 centimeters) in height. They thrive in partial shade or full sun in a temperate climate. Their blooming season is from July until the first frost.

Ageratum belongs to the composite family, and is related to thistles, marigolds, and bachelor's button. I. H. S.

SEE ALSO: COMPOSITE FLOWER, TRANSPLANTING

Ageratum, Blue cap

Ages of animals see Animals, life span

Ages of man see Evolution of man

Agglutination see Blood types

Aggregate see Concrete, Fruit, Rocks

Aging From the moment that a living organism comes into being it gradually undergoes the process of aging. Age is often measured by the time an organism has lived, but age is measured better by the amount of change that has taken place.

A living organism is active. It is this activity that produces the changes in the cells or tissues, recognized as aging. As the products of living activity accumulate gradually, they create slow changes in form and physiology.

In the human body, the egg that develops into a many-celled embryo is aging. After a baby is born, he or she continues to change into larger and more mature form as he or she ages. At about the age of 18 years, a person may reach the end of growth in overall size, but many changes are still taking place in the body's structure and functioning.

Signs of old age can often be seen easily. The skin becomes wrinkled and less flexible. The bones become brittle, break easily, and do not heal as readily. Muscles become weaker, softer, and smaller. There may be a loss of hair (baldness), particularly in men. The hair that remains turns to gray or white.

Certain diseases and body failures occur because different parts of the body begin to wear out. The arteries may harden with age and cause heart attacks or strokes to happen. Glandular ATROPHY, ARTHRITIS, and kidney disorders are some of the degenerative conditions that result from aging.

Geriatrics is a branch of medicine which deals with aging and the diseases of old age. J. D. B.

Farming is agriculture in practice. The buildings of a farm are adapted to the farmer's work

Agriculture There were only wild plants and animals in the world before this science began. Agriculture is the growing of plants and the raising of animals for man's needs. Early man wandered from place to place, finding food to eat when he needed it. Finally he started to sow seeds. He had to stay in one place at least until his crops were grown. This forced him to give up a nomad's life and settle. His first tools were wooden sticks to stir the soil. This was very primitive but it was the beginning of agriculture. It was born outside the cave of early man.

When the pioneer farmers began to settle down in America they raised many different kinds of crops. This was known as diversified farming. This type of agriculture was a necessity since transportation from one place to another took days or even weeks. The early farmer had to grow his own garden vegetables, raise cattle for meat, keep chickens for eggs, and cultivate a variety of crops to feed his livestock. Today this picture has changed considerably. Most farmers now specialize in one or two agricultural products. The improvement of transportation, the science of food preservation, and complexity of farm machinery have been instrumental in bringing about this change.

FARMING REVOLUTION

With the invention of machines less than 200 years ago, a great change came about in agriculture. The most successful early invention for speeding the harvesting of grain was the reaper patented by Cyrus McCormick of Chicago. Other horse and steam-driven machines, such as corn planters, cultivators, and threshing machines, were invented in rapid order. These machines increased production and decreased the number of laborers needed.

The invention of the gasoline ENGINE brought about a great change in agriculture. For many years, wagons and farm machinery were drawn by oxen, donkeys, or horses. The gasoline engine led to the replacement of animals with tractors and trucks. The modern combine reaps and threshes the grain and sacks it ready for milling into flour.

SCIENCE AND AGRICULTURE

Science has brought about a tremendous change, both in the life of farm families and in agricultural methods. Because one man is able to cultivate many acres with the use of modern machinery, small diversified farms are rapidly being replaced by large, mechanized, one-crop farms.

Modern machines do several jobs at once. They can turn the soil, apply fertilizer, and plant the seed all in one trip. These large machines can do ten to twelve rows at a time, unlike the older models that did two or four rows. But they are less accurate and efficient. Some places don't get planted because of the uneven terrain.

The scientific farmer calls upon and uses the services of scientists in other fields of knowledge. The chemist has developed new fertilizers. He has also produced various kinds of weed killers and insecticides. These greatly increase the per acre yield of crops for the farmer. He is now researching the use of chemicals that will open and close the stoma on the underside of leaves. When man controls the rate of transpiration by plants he can lick many drought problems.

The geologist is constantly working out new ways of improving the quality of the soil and finding better ways of conservation. Soil scientists analyze and make soil maps for farmers. Physicists are developing more efficient farm machinery. Geneticists are constantly experimenting on inbreeding and crossbreeding of plants and animals.

Researchers use electronic computers, radio-isotopes, aerial photography, and geophysical equipment to discover the nature and location of ground water. This research will lead to improved areas of cultivation and cut down on the runoff into the seas. Billions of dollars are currently being spent on watershed programs.

Even the aerospace scientists are contributing to agriculture. Hydroponics is farming plants without soil. Experiments in the space program are throwing much light on the kinds of plants and conditions for growth necessary in a solution of essential nutrients. Less and less farmland is available as the population increases. Man will be forced to perfect hydroponics as a common agricultural technique.

DANGERS TO THE LAND

Most of the land that can be used to grow crops is now under cultivation. Any new areas would mean moving out of the normal grassland BIOME and into others. Man could clear more forests, try to build up desert regions, or take over a jungle. However, disturbing these natural biomes would only eliminate other products needed by man and wreck the habitats of the animal and plant life that live in these areas.

Currently there are more than five billion people in the world to feed. This number is increasing by at least 2% each year. More than half the people in the world suffer from malnutrition. Although total food production has increased, there is a decrease in the amount of food available per person. In North America agricultural production has risen over 2% annually for several decades, but this food rarely reaches the malnourished people in other countries.

The population in many cities is decreasing as people move into the suburbs. This means that the farms surrounding the city are being turned into residential areas,

The growing of wheat is a wide-spread activity of agriculture in the United States. Wheat fields can be seen throughout large sections of the country. The sturdy wheat of today is the result of years of scientific research. Modern types resist disease and bad weather. Wheat farmers get a much larger yield per acre than they used to

John Deere

The ground is prepared by plowing. The stubble from the old crop becomes nourishment for the new. A modern grain drill sows the seeds which grow and become the beautiful wheat field shown at the left above

John Deere

Another section of the combine collects the kernels which flow into a truck for carting to the grain elevator. The remaining straw is used for feeding and bedding livestock

International Harvester

When the wheat is ripe, a combine crosses the field cutting and threshing the grain. Threshing removes the wheat kernel from the plant

U.S.D.A. Photo

Soil erosion endangers the land's fertility.

shopping centers, industrial complexes, and a maze of highways to transport people and things. Thousands of crop-producing acres are being covered up and lost forever. The polluters and pollutants are moving to the country.

The farmers surrounding these developments are plagued with smog and industrial wastes. Lead, mercury, and cadmium are just three of the heavy metal pollutants that accumulate in agricultural produce. Many small truck farms must be near large cities in order to get fresh produce in daily to market. Many wonder if their fruits and vegetables are safe to eat.

RESOURCES

There has also been a slow to rapid decline in soil fertility on the land that is available. Thousands of acres are now worn out and lost to farming. There is a constant removal of nutrients when single crops are raised on the same ground. The increased cost of fertilizer curtails the farmer from replacing 100% of those minerals removed each year, and the soil gradually wears out.

Plowing has many devastating effects upon soil. There is an increased rate of leaching—the moving of organic materials deeper into the ground, below the reaches of the crop roots. It exposes humus to the air where part of it is lost to oxidation. It increases soil erosion, especially when land is plowed in the fall and the bare ground is exposed to the winds until spring. It takes hundreds of years to make an inch (or 2.54 centimeters) of soil. Airborne soil eventually settles to earth. If it were carried from farm to farm it would not be lost. However, too much rich soil falls on cities, waterways, and areas where it is wasted and eventually carried away.

In many countries irrigation is used to make arid land productive. Often salt water is used. Most of this water is lost by evaporation or by transpiration. The salt remains, concentrations build up, and soon no plants can live in that soil.

The use of fertilizer is creating another problem. It washes off farm lands into ditches and often ends up polluting streams. Fertilizers cause water plants to grow and reproduce in such numbers that waterways become clogged with algal blooms. High concentrations of fertilizer are good for plant growth, but excess fertilizer is stored in their organs. Herbivores, including man, that eat plants loaded with such fertilizer elements as cobalt and copper become sick. Farmers have found that it is cheaper to stay with the artificial fertilizers than use the millions of tons of human sewage, animal wastes, and other organic refuse. Most of the latter must be buried or piled upon this already polluted earth.

FARMING PRACTICES TODAY

Farming today certainty isn't what it used to be. When a man pays $3,000 for an acre of ground instead of the $5 in the past, he wants to be sure he gets his money's worth from the soil. In the old days he husked corn by hand and threw it into a horse-drawn wagon. Now he invests in a $40,000+ corn combine. Farmers have turned to the knowledge of genetics to help them pick the kinds of plants and animals to raise. This science has produced some fantastic breeds of living things.

Inbreeding is the crossing of closely related organisms until they breed "true," such as the fine racehorses. Outbreeding is crossing organisms not closely related. This develops hybrid vigor. Mules and hybrid corn are both products of this latter. Farmers are interested in the following traits in plants and animals:

1. How much will they produce?

The amount of milk a cow gives, the number of ears on a stalk of corn, the quantity of fruit on a tree, the number of pigs in a litter—all these figures are important in mass production. The wild jungle fowl laid about 20 eggs a year. The present White Leghorn hen may lay over 200 per year.

2. What is the quality of the product?

The proportion of butterfat in milk, the kind of meat on a hog, the fineness of wool on a sheep, the color and size of fruits—all these traits are considered. Cattaloes (cross between cattle and buffaloes) produce a fine grade of meat while grazing on very poor pastureland.

3. What is the structure of organisms?

Farmers are interested in hornless cattle, in sheep with shorter legs, turkeys with bigger breast muscles, and vegetables with larger storage parts. The Rhode Island Reds and Plymouth Rock fowls may be 18 inches tall (45.72 centimeters) and weigh over 9 pounds (4.08 kilograms).

4. Are they resistant to diseases and to various disorders?

Constant in- and outbreeding is producing plants which cannot be damaged by fungus, bacteria, and virus. Stronger and healthier livestock are crossed with weaker types to produce the best traits of both in the offspring.

It is apparent that the science of genetics is playing an ever-increasing role in the area of agriculture. Selective breeding is producing better domesticated animals and plants of higher yield. Many are markedly different from their wild ancestors. Agriculture has come a long way since early man tamed his first dog and planted the first seed in the soil. There are many opportunities for young people today in the science of agriculture. It has become a real profession. The tillers of the soil have come of age. H. J. C.

SEE ALSO: BACTERIA, BIOME, CONSERVATION, EROSION, FOOD PRESERVATION, HORTICULTURE, MACHINERY.

Agronomy The branch of agriculture that deals with the theory and art of field crop production and soil management is called agronomy. It is also the theory and practice of growing plants so that the fertility of the soil is conserved.

In the middle 1890's the term "agronomy" was introduced into the agricultural colleges and experimental stations. These stations do a vast amount of experimental work and research. The results are published in pamphlets and bulletins for free distribution.

The cultivation of plants depends on soil, water, and climate. Constant watchfulness for injurious plant pests and diseases is necessary. The study of agronomy teaches us how to battle the adverse conditions that prevent good plant growth.

Agricultural chemistry is required for the study of SOIL fertility and composition of plants. Maintenance of soil fertility is accomplished by proper rotation or succession of crops because different crops make different demands upon the soil. Legumes like ALFALFA and SOYBEANS enrich soil because of nitrogen-fixing bacteria within their roots. Often the entire crop of legumes is plowed under the soil. W. J. K.

AIDS see Acquired Immune Deficiency Syndrome

Air Man lives at the bottom of an ocean of air. Life depends on air. Animals need oxygen from the air to live. Air is a mixture of gases, about 78% nitrogen, 21% oxygen, and small amounts of other gases. In addition, air contains vapor and a wide assortment of small particles, such as dust, soot, and salt, as well as pollen grains, spores, and bacteria.

Air extends great distances above the earth, but one-half of the air by weight is within 3½ miles (5.63 kilometers) of the earth's surface. The other half is spread over hundreds of miles above that.

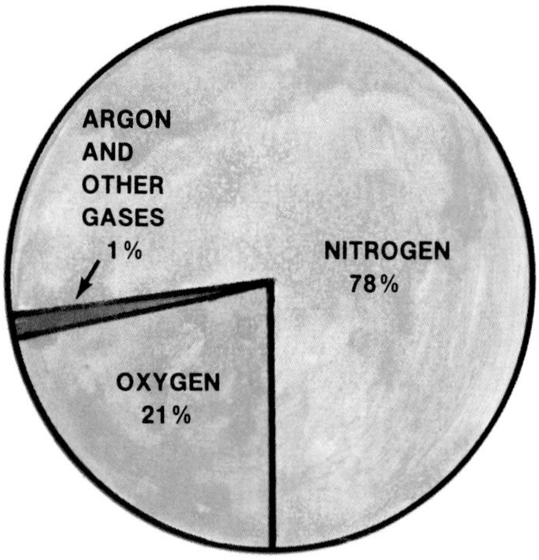

COMPOSITION OF AIR

Nitrogen and oxygen make up 98% of air. But some of the gases found in trace amounts are also very important. Carbon dioxide greatly influences the *greenhouse effect* in the lower portion of the atmosphere. It is this effect that helps retain heat energy received from the sun.

The greenhouse effect can also be dangerous to the earth's overall climate. In the greenhouse effect short-wave radiation passes through the earth's atmosphere. This radiation is then absorbed by surface materials and reradiated back into space as long-wave heat radiation. The atmosphere will not permit long-wave radiation to pass through. The atmosphere acts as an insulation trapping the heat. This process could eventually cause a global rise in temperature. This in turn would melt the icecaps and raise ocean levels. A greenhouse effect can start by natural means, such as volcanic eruptions, or through man-made pollutants being suspended in the upper atmosphere.

The ozone layer prevents most of the sun's ultraviolet radiation from reaching the surface of the earth. This is the type of radiation that causes sunburn. If it were not for the ozone layer, we would have to protect ourselves from the direct rays of the sun at all times. The percentage composition of the air considers only the gases of the atmosphere and does not include two other important ingredients, water vapor and the many different types of dust—without either one, precipitation would never occur. The amount of water vapor in the air varies greatly from time to time and from place to place. Dust in the air serves as condensation nuclei around which water vapor can condense. The source of this dust may be dust storms, combustion products from the exhaust of automobiles, and smoke

✳ **THINGS TO DO**

DOES AIR TAKE UP SPACE?

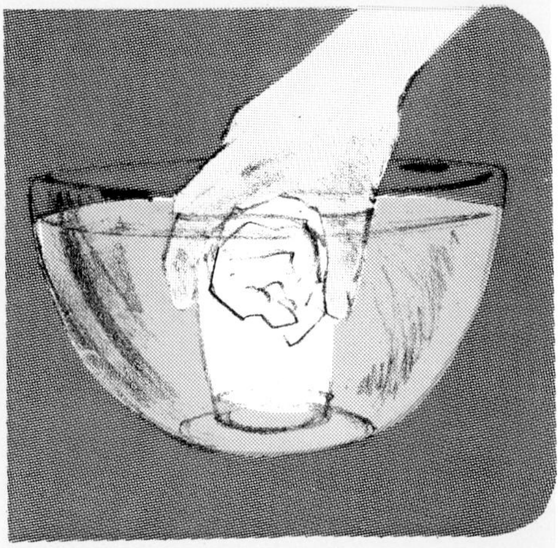

1 Crumple up a sheet of paper and push it into the bottom of a drinking glass.

2 Turn the glass over and push it straight down into a large jar or bowl of water.

3 Does the paper get wet?

4 If the experiment has been done properly, the air surrounding the paper cannot change places with the water.

✳ **THINGS TO DO**

DOES AIR TAKE UP SPACE?

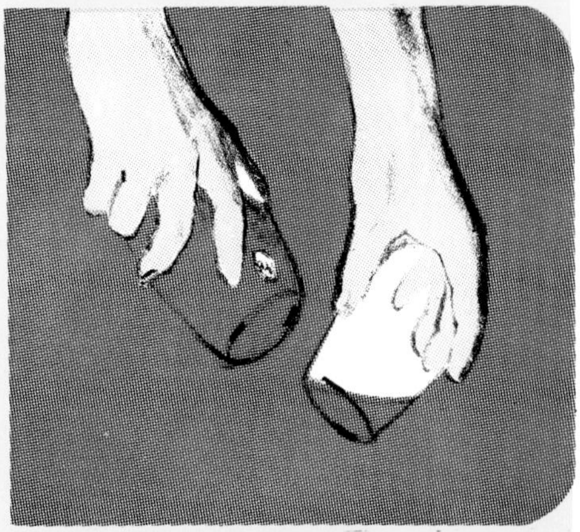

1 Turn two glasses upside down and push them below the surface of the water in an aquarium.

2 Tilt one glass to permit it to fill with water. Hold the two glasses near each other with the rim of the glass of air slightly below the rim of the other glass.

3 Now tilt the glass of air to allow the air to escape. It will go into the glass of water.

4 As this second glass catches the bubbles, what happens to the water?

from factories. Dust from massive volcanic eruptions causes spectacular red sunsets which may last for several years. Dust also includes plant pollen, bacteria, and tiny salt particles that are thrown into the air from the breaking waves of the oceans.

The air that surrounds the earth may be divided into layers or zones. In meteorology, four layers, based on temperature changes, are generally considered. Extending up from the earth to about 7 miles (11.27 kilometers) altitude is the *troposphere*, the zone where most of the earth's weather occurs. Above this are the *stratosphere, mesosphere,* and finally the *thermosphere,* where the air thins out into space.

AIR PRESSURE

The force of GRAVITY holds the air around the earth and gives it weight. At SEA LEVEL one cubic foot of air weighs only .081 pounds (.04 kilograms), but the hundreds of miles of air above the earth weigh so much that the total force on 1 square foot of surface is about 2100 pounds or 14.7 pounds per square inch (760 millimeters of mercury as read on a barometer). This force on a given area is called AIR PRESSURE.

Air pressure at the earth's surface is equal in all directions so that we are unaware of this enormous pressure of more than a ton per square foot. At an altitude of 18,000 feet (5486.4 meters), the pressure is still at least one-half as great. For this reason airplanes and spacecraft have pressurized cabins to make flying more comfortable for the people.

Molecules of air are in constant motion, and since they are perfectly elastic no energy is lost when they collide with each other or with the walls of any container. Air may be compressed and used in automobile tires. The constant force of the air molecules striking the tire walls keeps the tire from going flat. In summer, air molecules in a tire become warmer and move faster, increasing the pressure in the tire.

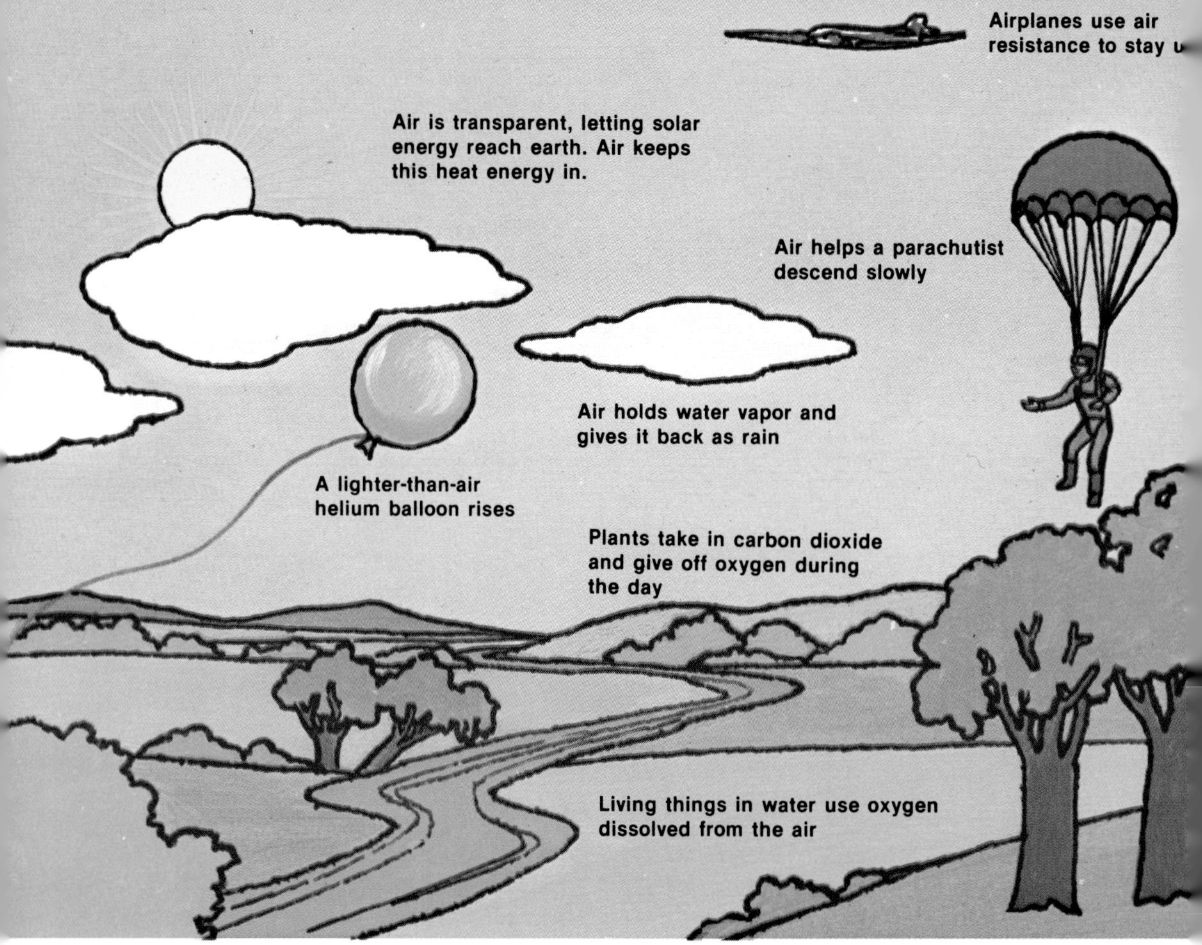
Airplanes use air resistance to stay u
Air is transparent, letting solar energy reach earth. Air keeps this heat energy in.
Air helps a parachutist descend slowly
Air holds water vapor and gives it back as rain
A lighter-than-air helium balloon rises
Plants take in carbon dioxide and give off oxygen during the day
Living things in water use oxygen dissolved from the air

Air is not very dense, and we move through it without difficulty. But when a jet moves through it at high speed, air offers considerable resistance. Large masses of air offer much resistance, too. This permits a parachute to descend slowly, because the large volume of air under it cannot be moved rapidly by the weight of the parachute and the man.

OTHER CHARACTERISTICS OF AIR

Air is colorless, odorless, and tasteless. Large quantities of air are dissolved in the water of the oceans, lakes, and rivers. The air in water provides oxygen for fish and other forms of life in water.

Air exerts a bouyant force on all objects surrounded by it, just as water exerts BUOYANCY. However, the buoyant force of air is very small because of its light weight. When a balloon filled with hydrogen or helium rises in the air, it does so because these gases weigh less than the air the balloon displaces. The buoyant effect on an average-sized person is only about one-fifth of a pound.

The ability of air to absorb water vapor helps in the distribution of solar energy received by the earth. Warm air can hold more water vapor than cold air. Heat is required to evaporate water. Moisture-laden air from tropical lands may be blown by the wind to distant points where it is much cooler. As the air is cooled, it releases the water vapor as rain. When water vapor turns back to water, it releases all the heat energy it originally absorbed. The wind system alone helps to distribute heat energy, too. Air, like most substances, expands when heated and becomes lighter or less dense. Unequal heating of the earth over land and water sets up currents of air or wind. Cooler air is more dense and exerts more pressure than warmer air and tends to push warmer air to other regions. Wind directions are influenced by the earth's rotation, too.

SEE ALSO: AIR MASSES, AIR POLLUTION, ATMOSPHERE, GAS, GREENHOUSE EFFECT, OZONE, SKY, WEATHER

Air brakes see Brakes

Air column see Sound

Air compressor see Compressors

Air conditioning Air conditioning alters the air in buildings and homes to make indoor conditions more comfortable and healthful. In industry, air conditioning also includes controlling atmospheric conditions for efficiently carrying out various manufacturing processes.

In summer, air may be cooled, dried and cleaned. In winter, it may be warmed, moistened, cleaned, and filtered. Air conditioning keeps air in motion, too, for ventilation. Odors may be removed. The air is dried or moistened to make the HUMIDITY ideal for comfort. Long before air conditioning machines were developed, attempts to humidify the air in heated rooms depended upon evaporation of water in pans or the spraying of water into the air.

Warm air can take up more water vapor than cold air can. When air is heated indoors, it can hold much more water vapor. If additional water is not used, the relative humidity drops. The water present may fall to 10%. People are more comfortable when it is from 30% to 50%. The air conditioner adds more water. In summer, the air indoors is generally too moist—often 80% to 95% water vapor. Then the air conditioner removes moisture to bring the humidity down to 50% or less. This moisture is usually removed by cooling the air with refrigerating coils. As the air is cooled, moisture condenses and freezes on the coils.

Amana Refrigeration, Inc.

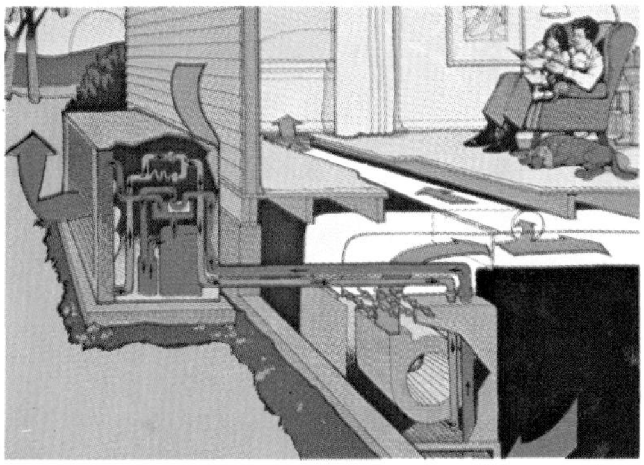

An air conditioner moves cool air into a house and heated air to the outside.

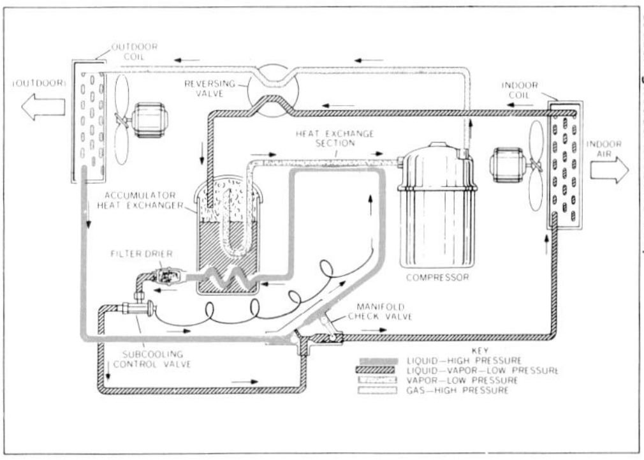

Westinghouse Electric Corp

Diagram showing the heating and cooling of Freon in a modern air conditioning unit.

Today air conditioning machines are available for single rooms, entire houses, large theaters and buildings, and huge industrial plants. These machines may heat or cool the air, add or remove moisture, clean or actually wash the air, filter it, and circulate it with a gentle motion.

The usual home air conditioner is a refrigerator that cools the air in a house. Liquified gas, usually Freon-12, is passed through an expansion valve where it is vaporized and greatly cooled. The cooled Freon goes into a coil of pipes. Warm air is cooled when blown over the cool pipes with the Freon taking on the heat from the air. The Freon runs into a compressor and its pressure and temperature are increased substantially. The Freon passes next into a second coil outside. In the second coil the Freon gives off heat and is converted to a liquid. By completing this cycle an air conditioner pumps heat from inside to outside.

J. H. D. / A. J. H.

SEE ALSO: AIR POLLUTION, OZONE

Air hammer An air hammer is a tool used for such work as breaking concrete. A piston is pushed back and forth by compressed air, making the hammer strike. TOOLS that work by air are called PNEUMATIC tools.

Air lock An air lock is an airtight compartment in which the AIR PRESSURE can be changed. It permits workmen to adjust gradually to high pressures.

SEE: BENDS, DECOMPRESSION

Air masses When the weather man talks about tomorrow's weather, he is describing the possible results of the movements of large parcels of air. These air masses form over areas of land or water. As heat is added to or taken from them, it sets up a series of actions and reactions which account for our weather.

An air mass is a body of air extending over a large area, usually 1,000+ miles (1,609+ kilometers) or more across, with fairly uniform properties horizontally. That is, layer for layer, the air in one part of the air mass has about the same characteristics as the air in other parts of the same mass. The basic properties of an air mass are its temperature and its moisture.

Air masses are either cold or warm regardless of the season of the year. A cold air mass is colder than the ground surface over which it flows. Warm air masses are warmer than the surface over which they move.

A cold air mass is denser than a warm air mass. One cubic foot of cold air weighs more than the same quantity of warm air. Thus a cold air mass exerts greater pressure on the earth than a warm air mass. Cooler air tends to move toward the warmer air because of the difference in pressure.

Air masses are so huge that when a cold air mass meets a warm one, it tends to run under the warm air instead of mixing with the warm air. In doing so, it elevates or pushes up the warm air. The line along which this occurs is called a *cold front.* As the warm air is pushed up, it expands and cools causing cloud formations and PRECIPITATION such as rain or snow. Precipitation occurs because cooled air cannot hold as much water vapor as it did before cooling.

In like manner, if wind movements cause a warm air mass to over-take a cold air mass, the warm air, being less dense, slides up over the cold and forms clouds and precipitation, too. This condition is called a *warm front.*

The weather over a location at a given time generally depends on either the character of the prevailing air mass, or the interaction of two or more air masses. Except where this interaction is taking place, the weather is somewhat similar throughout an area covered by the same air mass, with variations caused by local geographical features such as lakes, mountains, and valleys.

When a body of air comes to rest or moves very slowly over a land or sea area that has uniform characteristics of temperature and moisture, the mass tends to take on the same uniform properties—the coldness of polar regions or the heat of the tropics or the moisture of the oceans or the dryness of the continents.

The region where an air mass acquired its particular characteristics of temperature and moisture is called its "source region." The depth to which an air mass becomes modified by its source region depends upon (1) the length of the time the air remains in the source region, and (2) the difference between the original temperature of the air and that of the underlying surface.

Weather maps use letter symbols to identify air masses. They indicate not only the source of origin of a mass of air, but the direction in which it is moving and the characteristics of the surface over which it is traveling. The air mass first assumes the characteristics of the area over which it originates. A continental air mass (c) is dry; a tropical air mass (T) is hot; a maritime air mass (m) is humid; and a polar air mass (P) is cold. However, as it travels, its characteristics are changed by the nature of the surface over which it passes. As an air mass moves from one surface to another it could change from a warm air mass (w) to a cold air mass (k), or just the reverse.

Across the United States the general movement is eastward. A cold air mass moves more rapidly than a warm one, sometimes averaging from 500-700 miles (804-1126 kilometers) in a day, depending upon its own nature and the season of the year. E.M.N.

SEE ALSO: CYCLONE, HIGH PRESSURE CENTER, LOW PRESSURE CENTER, WEATHER FORECASTING

Air pollution Air is a mixture of gases. There is air pollution when man adds substances to the air that cause damage. The added substances may be either solids or gases. They can damage either man's health or the environment.

Air pollution has been a major problem for at least three centuries. In cities pollution has caused mankind considerable discomfort. The pollutants can be separated into two major groups; particulate matter and gases.

Particulate matter (solid or liquid) is matter divided into small particles. The size of particles ranges from the very large dust particles down to small molecules and viruses. Included in these particles are tobacco smoke, auto exhaust, pollen, and sea salt particles. The smaller particles enter into the lungs where they damage the lung tissue.

Sulfur oxides are the end products of burning sulfur and form acids when dissolved in rain. These acids damage plant and animal tissues and the environment. Carbon monoxide and carbon dioxide are produced by decaying and burning fuels. Carbon monoxide is highly poisonous to animals. High concentrations of carbon dioxide may cause climate changes. Nitrogen oxides are produced by the high temperature combustion of fuels. Nitrogen oxides are produced in automobiles. The oxides of nitrogen produce acids when dissolved in rain, and react like the oxides of sulfur.

Other pollutants found in the air are lead, produced by auto emissions; ozone, produced by photo-chemical reactions; hydrocarbons, produced by incomplete burning of fuels; and freons, the propellants used in aerosol cans and in refrigeration devices. A.J.H.

SEE ALSO: CARBON MONOXIDE, GREENHOUSE EFFECT, HYDROCARBON, OZONE

Air pressure It is easy to feel the force of air when one is standing in the wind. It is not so easy, though, to realize that all air, even when very still, has weight and pushes against everything around it. Realizing this is more difficult because AIR is a gas and it is invisible. Its particles, or molecules, are not as dense, or closely spaced, as are the particles which make up the ground. However, air does have weight, just as does water and rock.

The pressure of the air is caused by the weight of the air molecules that make up the atmosphere of the earth. The average air pressure at sea level is 14.7 pounds per square inch (1.03 kilograms per square centimeter). Air pressure is transmitted in all directions. Changes in the temperature of the air as well as the relative humidity bring about changes in the air pressure. Air pressure is measured with a mercury BAROMETER or with an aneroid barometer. E.M.N.

SEE ALSO: AERODNAMICS; FLIGHT, PRINCIPALS OF; PRESSURE

THINGS TO DO

WILL AIR PUSH AN EGG INTO A BOTTLE?

Materials: milk bottle, hard-boiled egg with shell removed, match, paper

1 Crumple a sheet of paper and drop it into a milk bottle. Light the end of a paper straw. Hold the burning end in the bottle until the paper catches on fire. Let the paper burn until the flame goes out. Set the egg over the opening of the bottle. Watch what happens to the egg. What is pushing the egg into the bottle? Why?

Air resistance Air resistance is the force exerted by air against any object moving in it. The air exerts this force because it has weight.

SEE: AERODYNAMICS; FLIGHT, PRINCIPLES OF; PRESSURE

Air traffic control see Aviation

Air transportation see Aviation

Aircraft The term aircraft in its broadest sense means any craft designed to carry man into the atmosphere. Today, heavier-than-air craft are built in all sizes and shapes, depending upon how they are to be used. Lighter-than-air craft refers to balloons and airships.

The advantages of the airplane include high-speed travel and almost complete freedom from land barriers, such as rivers, mountains, oceans, and deserts.

Legend and history have told of man's attempt to copy bird flight by building flapping mechanical wings. These muscle-powered devices all failed. About 200 years ago, hot air balloons enabled man to float into the air. These craft evolved into the cigar-shaped, propeller-driven airships that were used for long-distance travel. Several disasters, plus the advance of heavier-than-air craft, ended the commercial value of the airship in the mid-1930s.

HEAVIER-THAN-AIR CRAFT

Another approach to mastering the problems of flight was taken during the period of airship development. The first heavier-than-air craft were gliders, often pushed off of hilltops. The first successful powered flight was achieved on December 17, 1903, at Kitty Hawk, North Carolina. The flimsy machine was propelled about 100 feet (30.48 meters) by a home-built gasoline engine, connected by bicycle chains to two wooden propellers. This brief flight was the climax of many years' effort by two American brothers, Orville and Wilbur Wright. Within a decade, flying machines and techniques of control were advanced to the point where the airplane became useful. World War I brought more advances, including multi-engined aircraft and those designed for special purposes.

Aeronautical science has progressed rapidly. The development of new power plants, structural materials, and electronic devices have made reliable aircraft available for transportation of people and cargo. The aircraft industry is constantly producing vehicles capable of greater speed and greater load-carrying capabilities.

Aircraft may be divided into many types and classifications, depending upon their use. Some are small with a single engine. Others are huge multi-engined machines.

COMMERCIAL AIRLINERS

The introduction of large passenger liners and fuel-efficient jet engines has helped more people fly inexpensively than ever before possible. Some aspects of commercial aviation, however, have changed little over the last three decades. Today's jet airliners cruise at about the same speed, 550 miles (885 kilometers) per hour, as those in service in the late 1950s. In the late 1950s, as well as in the 1990s, most commercial airliners flew at heights up to 40,000 feet (12,192 meters). An exception is the European Concorde, which is capable of flying at nearly twice the SPEED OF SOUND and at heights up to 70,000 feet (21,336 meters).

In the United States, the commercial airline industry was changed dramatically in 1984. The government disbanded the Civil Aeronautics Board, which controlled the routes airlines flew and the rates they charged. In some cases, increased competition led to lower prices. Unfortunately, some airline companies were bankrupted.

Many of the most dramatic changes in airliners today involve electronic navigation and safety equipment. Despite increasingly heavy traffic at major airports (O'Hare Field in Chicago serves more than 50,000,000 passengers each year), computer-assisted equipment has helped commercial flying remain one of the safest methods of long-distance travel available.

MILITARY AIRCRAFT

Powered aircraft have been used in military conflicts since World War I. The devastating power of modern military aircraft was shown during the 1991 Persian Gulf War. During the brief conflict, American F-117A Stealth fighters proved to be virtually invisible on Iraqi RADAR. Aircraft were equipped with weapons, called smart bombs, that were guided to their targets by LASER beams with precision never before possible. High-flying reconnaissance aircraft helped to monitor all aspects of the battles.

Most of the sophisticated military aircraft in use today were developed in the United States, the former Soviet Union, France, and

U.S. Navy

Courtesy U.S. Air Force

The Boeing Company

By tilting its turbofans, the Grumman Design 598 (left), a V/STOL, can have both forward thrust and up-and-down control. The F1-17 (top), which flew "invisibly" in the 1991 Persian Gulf War. The new Boeing 777 (bottom) is due to be in the air before 1995; it will seat as many as 440 passengers.

Great Britain. They include small, fast fighters, such as the Russian MiG 25, the French Mirage, the British Harrier (capable of vertical landings and takeoffs), and the American F15A and F-16. All these fighters can fly at speeds of at least twice the speed of sound. Larger craft, called bombers, are capable of carrying massive bombs and other heavy weapons over long distances. Bombers capable of traveling at twice the speed of sound include the Russian Backfire, and the American FB-111A and recently developed B-1.

Other types of military aircraft include helicopters, cargo and troop carriers, and various types of rocket-powered MISSILES.

R.T.T./D.D./J.H.

LIGHT AIRCRAFT

This category represents the largest number of aircraft being flown today, 506,509 in 1983. It includes the small two- to eight-passenger airplane, which is typically privately owned and is flown for business and pleasure. The Federal Aviation Administration defines these aircraft as weighing under 12,500 pounds (5,669.9 kilograms). The light plane has one- or two-piston propeller type engines, which provide cruising airspeeds between 100 and 300 miles (160.93-482.8 kilometers) per hour. The recent availability of small, more powerful turboprop engines, however, is making larger and faster light twin-engine aircraft available.

Light aircraft are designed to be easily flown by the nonprofessional, as well as the professional pilot. Adequate instruments and radio navigation equipment are usually available to permit flight during adverse weather conditions. The pilot, however, must be specifically trained in the use of these instruments and be properly licensed before he can take full advantage of the aircraft's capability.

The landing gear of light aircraft may retract into the wings or fuselage or remain in a permanent position. Skis or floats may be added for operation on snow or water.

An increasing number of individuals are building their own airplanes to be flown for sport. The Experimental Aircraft Association has become a source of information and encouragement. The craftsmanship required has become a challenge, even to many nonpilots.

Gliders and *sailplanes* are used for flying. Since they have no engine they must be towed aloft by a power plane or launched by an auto tow or winch. Once released, they sustain aerodynamic flight by gliding. By maneuvering within rising air currents or thermals, flights up to several hours are possible.

Cessna Aircraft Co.

This single-engine aircraft, the first high-wing on the market, has retractable landing gear

V/STOL AIRCRAFT

V/STOL is the abbreviation for Vertical or Short Takeoff and Landing aircraft. Helicopters or rotary wing aircraft are the most common type of V/STOLS used. Large propeller-like rotors are mounted above the fuselage and generate vertical lift when rapidly rotated by the engine. Horizontal movement is achieved by tilting the rotor and changing the pitch of the rotor blades. Helicopters are extremely versatile and have become increasingly important for both industrial and military tasks.

The autogyro is also a rotary wing aircraft; however, its rotor blades are not driven by the engine. Forward thrust is provided by a conventional propeller. The movement of the autogyro through the air causes the blades to rotate, and subsequently lift is generated.

Considerable attention is now being given to the development of V/STOL aircraft. The military is especially concerned by the increasing runway requirements of its high-performance jet aircraft. Several approaches have reached the test-flight stage, while others are still engineers' concepts. *Variable geometry* is a term describing the design where the position of the wing can be changed. The most desirable lift and airflow characteristics are provided in both low- and high-speed flight. Improved airfoil designs, improved laminar flow techniques, and high lift devices are also under investigation.

Another design approach is the *tilt wing.* The entire wing, including the turboprop engines, is rotated to a vertical position for takeoff. Once airborne, the wing is gradually rotated to the conventional horizontal position where the propellers provide forward thrust.

Some V/STOL aircraft simply direct the jet engine thrust downward to achieve vertical lift. Others divert the jet engine exhaust to drive large lift fans imbedded in the fuselage and wings, providing vertical thrust for takeoff and landing.

Ground effect machines or GEMS can be classified as aircraft since they are supported above the ground by a bubble of compressed air. Large fans maintain the bubble. The vehicle travels over the earth's surface, including water at heights ranging from a few inches to a few feet. GEMS are now being used as military combat vehicles.

Research vehicles have utilized the tremendous power of rocket engines to achieve speeds approaching 5,000 mph (8046.72 kilometers per hour) and altitudes of over 50 miles (80.47 kilometers).

True aerospace craft, called *lifting bodies,* gain lift from the shape of their fuselages, not their wings. These have led to development of the Space Shuttle. In space, these shuttles obey the laws of orbital mechanics, but on re-entry into Earth's atmosphere they are subject to laws of aerodynamics, and can be guided to land on long conventional runways, like massive gliders.

R.T.T./D.D./J.H.

SEE ALSO: AIR-CUSHION VEHICLE; AUTOGYRO; AVIATION; DIRIGIBLE; FLIGHT, PRINCIPLES OF; JET PROPULSION

CH-54 Sky Crane

U.S. Army

Aircraft carrier see Ships
Airfoil see Airplane
Airline see Aviation

Air-cushion vehicles The air-cushion vehicle is a machine that travels on a cushion of air a few inches above the ground. The machine may look like an automobile without wheels. The cushion of air is pushed out of the bottom of the machine by a large fan.

Air-cushion vehicles are sometimes called "ground effect machines." They usually have a rectangular shape with vertical duct openings for the fans or blowers imbedded within the machine. Engines are built into the top of the machine to provide power for the fans. Air is compressed by the fans and forced downward through ducts in the lower portion of the air-cushion vehicle.

There are two general types of air-cushion vehicles, those with an open chamber, and the peripheral jet type. The open chamber vehicles are completely open at the bottom. The compressed air from the blower is trapped in this chamber, and makes a cushion, or bubble, between the machine and the ground. It is this bubble that supports the vehicle. The peripheral jet type is closed at the bottom, but a slot runs all the way around the edge of the bottom. The air is forced out of this slot. It forms a cushion under the machine between the closed bottom and the ground. It also acts as an air "fence" to keep the cushion from leaking away too fast. The air does leak out from beneath the machine, but it is replaced by more air from the blower.

An extra engine and propeller is used on some vehicles to propel them forward. Many of the smaller ones are steered simply by shifting the weight of the driver around the

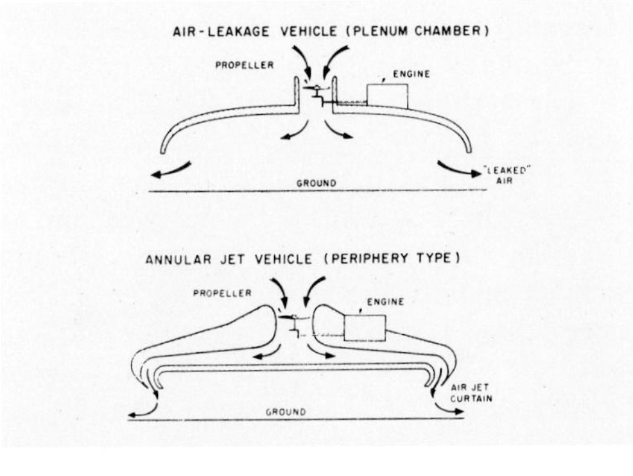

Hovermarine, Ltd.

Air-cushion vehicles are used to transport passengers and cargo on land or sea.

British Hovercraft Corporation

vehicle. Larger vehicles are steered by rudders like those on airplanes.

Air-cushion cars are useful over land, water, ice, snow, and mud. They travel between 1 inch and 3 feet (2.54-91.44 centimeters) off the ground, and can ride over any surface which is free of large obstacles. They have obtained speeds of over 70 mph (112.65 kilometers per hour.)

Air-cushion "trucks" can be used as amphibians to transport cargo from ships that are too large to dock close to shore.

Since air-cushion cars need no roads, and may travel over rivers and open country, they may be used to explore many uninhabited areas of the world. In the future, countries may only have to clear and level the land in order to use the air-cushion car for all of their transportation. They would have no need for a system of paved roads.

Military missions considered for the air-cushion vehicle include anti-submarine warfare, landing, patrol and rescue operations, mine countermeasures, and high-speed transport of personnel and cargo.

The transportation industry in the United States and Great Britain is already building air-cushion vehicles. Scheduled passenger service in the United States began on August 10, 1966, in the San Francisco-Oakland Bay area. R. J. J.

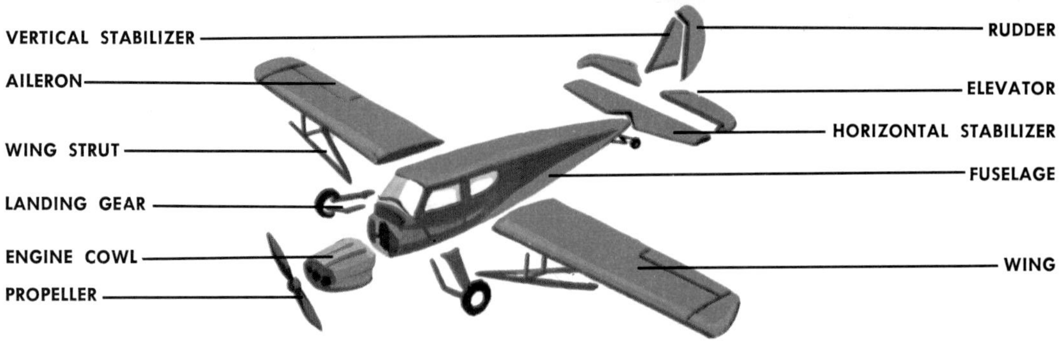

Principal parts of an airplane

Airplane Airplanes are powered aircraft. They are the most common type of flying vehicle.

Airplanes vary in size and purpose, yet they all have the same main parts. Every type of airplane has a main body, or *fuselage,* in which to carry the crew, controls, passengers, and cargo; *wings* to lift it into the air; a tail *assembly* to control the attitude of the aircraft; *landing gear* to give it mobility on the ground; and one or more *engines* for power to fly.

The airplane fuselage is designed for the particular type of cargo it will carry. The airliner has a long, cylindrical fuselage, and, because it is designed to carry passengers, has many windows. Cargo airplanes have very large bodies and often have loading doors in the rear for handling bulky loads. Private airplanes, like automobiles, have fuselages designed to carry one or more people, including the pilot. High performance military airplanes, such as fighters and bombers, have very streamlined fuselages designed to carry weapons and electronic equipment.

The airplane's wings are designed to generate *lift.* Depending upon the placement of the wings, an airplane is known as a high, low, or mid-wing type. Cargo and passenger airplanes have long, narrow wings, capable of lifting heavy loads, while jetliners and military airplanes usually have the swept back wings necessary for high speed flight. Some fighters and experimental airplanes have very short, straight, razor-sharp wings. Triangular or "delta" wings offer the streamlining necessary for high speeds, and yet permit good low-speed performance.

The *tail section* provides both the in-flight *control* of the airplane, and *stabilizes* it like the feathers of an arrow. Control is accomplished by moveable parts known as the *rudder* and the *elevators.* The rudder is hinged to the fixed vertical fin. When it is moved to the left or right by the pilot, it causes the nose of the airplane to yaw. The horizontal stabilizers are fixed with hinged elevators attached. Their movement pitches the nose of the airplane up or down. Hinged controls in the wings called *ailerons* cause the airplane to bank or roll to the side. Some airplanes have two or three vertical fins to increase stability. The horizontal stabilizer may be mounted on the fuselage or on the vertical fin.

Airplanes are equipped with landing gear to give them mobility on the ground. This usually consists of wheels attached to the fuselage (or wings) by struts. Airplanes may have the so-called "conventional" landing gear, with two main wheels near the front of the fuselage, and one small wheel at the tail. Very popular today is the *tricycle* landing gear, with two wheels at the middle of the fuselage, and one under the nose. *Tandem* type landing gear is used on heavy bombers. The wheels are mounted one behind the other under the fuselage with small wheels extended from the wings to keep the airplane from tipping. SEAPLANES use boatlike floats, or have watertight hulls for landing on the water. For winter flying, skis may replace the landing wheels.

There are two basic types of airplane engines. The *piston engine* was used by the Wright brothers, and is still in use today. Piston engines are similar to automobile ENGINES, and are connected to propellers to generate *thrust.* The *turbojet* engine was developed for aircraft use during World War II. The turbojet is of great significance because of its light weight, simple operation, and tremendous power. *Turboprop* engines use propellers as well as the jet principle to drive the airplane forward. They are actually turbojet engines the power of which is harnessed to a propeller. The ROCKET ENGINE is a type of jet engine which carries its own oxygen supply. It is capable of operating at

✳ THINGS TO DO

MAKING AN AIRPLANE MODEL WITH MOVING PARTS

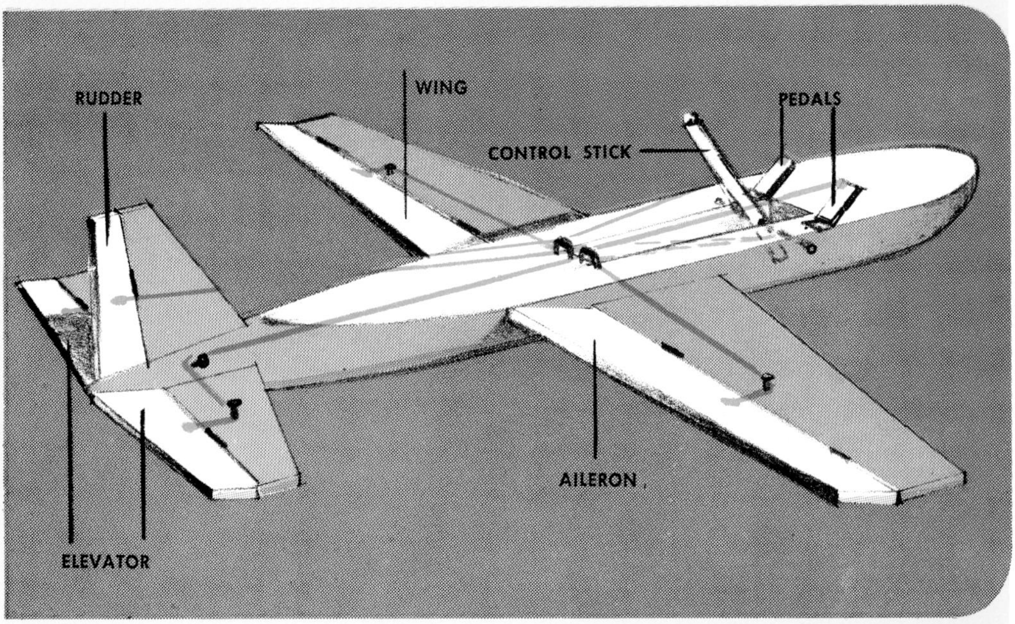

Materials: balsa wood, wire, screws, hinges, stick, wooden pedals

1 **Assemble an airplane by following the labeled illustration. The elevators, rudder, and ailerons are fastened to the body of the plane with small metal double hinges. With a stiff wire connect the right pedal to the right side of the rudder. Repeat on the left side. Fasten wire from the control stick to each aileron and elevator.**

2 **When the stick is pulled back the elevators are pulled up. The plane begins to climb. When the stick is moved to the right, the right aileron turns up and the left one goes down. The airplane turns right.**

3 **Experiment with the model airplane to understand how a pilot can use the controls to climb, nose-dive, bank to the right and to the left.**

tremendous speeds and altitudes, and is being used to carry man into space in the Space Shuttle. Spacecraft launch vehicles, such as the Saturn V, also use rocket engines.

Airplanes are basically simple to fly. Regardless of size or shape, the basic techniques are used. The control stick (or wheel), the rudder pedals, and the throttle are the three main controls. The *control stick* and *rudder pedal* movements are coordinated to turn the airplane by moving both in the direction of the desired turn. The airplane is prevented from gaining or losing altitude in its maneuvers by using forward or back pressure on the control stick, thus operating the elevators.

The airplane climbs or glides as the engine speed is changed by the *throttle.* Increasing the engine speed causes the airplane to speed up. Thus the wings generate more lift, and the airplane climbs. By reducing power, forward speed and lift are also reduced, and the airplane glides.

The *cockpit* is equipped with instruments which give the pilot information on position and course, rate of climb, angle of bank, altitude, and the operation of his engine. In addition to the other controls, there are switches to operate the other systems of the airplane. Almost all airplanes today have hydraulic systems to operate landing gear, brakes and other devices; electrical systems for lighting and radios; heaters and de-icing equipment and radio navigation devices.

R. J. J.

SEE ALSO: AERODYNAMICS; AIRCRAFT; AVIATION; FLIGHT, PRINCIPLES OF; INSTRUMENT LANDING SYSTEM; INSTRUMENT PANEL; JET PROPULSION

Airport see Aviation

The *Mayflower* is Goodyear's operational blimp. It is often seen at sports events. Goodyear

Airships Airships are lighter-than-air craft or vehicles. Nearly 200 years ago men first floated into the air in cloth balloons. The passengers rode in a basket tied to the ends of a net placed over the top half of the balloon. These early airships were first filled with hot air and later with a gas called HYDROGEN. As these balloons rose into the air, they were at the mercy of the winds and could not be steered.

The first controllable balloon or DIRIGIBLE was flown a distance of 17 miles (27.36 kilometers) in 1852 by a French clockmaker. It carried a small, three-horsepower steam engine connected to a propeller. Soon many men were building dirigibles. Perhaps the most famous was Count von Zeppelin of Germany, who built his first airship in 1898. He was later honored by having the German dirigibles named *Zeppelins.* The largest Zeppelin, the *Hindenburg,* was 803 feet (244.75 meters) long. It was propelled at a speed of about 85 miles (136.8 kilometers) per hour by four powerful diesel engines.

Almost all airships used today are much smaller and are called *blimps.* Early airships dropped *ballast* to make the aircraft rise, and they released small amounts of gas to descend. This procedure was later replaced by the addition of vertical and horizontal fins on the dirigibles.

Larger gas envelopes were cigar-shaped to reduce wind resistance. Two new types of gas bags which came into use were called *non-rigid* and *rigid.* The non-rigid type has several smaller balloons inside the large shell or envelope. The rigid type has a framework over which the gas envelope is placed. The envelope retains its shape, even without gas in it.

Germany led the world in construction of dirigibles. Eighty-eight rigid Zeppelins were built and flown during World War I. Many could carry loads of over 40 tons (36.29 metric tons) at speeds of 80 miles (128.75 kilometers) per hour. Great Britain and France produced smaller non-rigid airships called blimps which were used primarily for coastal patrol and submarine spotting.

The commercial future of the giant German Zeppelins looked promising following World War I. A series of crashes due to limitations of structural materials, weather forecasting, and the use of dangerous hydrogen gas was climaxed on May 6, 1937, with the tremendous burning of the *Hindenburg.* The decline of the use of the airship was also brought about by the rapid development of the airplane.

In 1976 as the result of studies conducted

at NASA's Ames Research Center at Moffett Field, California, two concepts for future dirigibles emerged. One, 200 feet long (60.96 meters), would carry 80 passengers at 176 miles (283.28 kilometers) per hour as a feeder airliner, taking off and landing vertically and powered with four tilting turboprop engines. Another, called the Heavy Lifter, combines features of large dirigibles and helicopter-type rotors, with a payload estimated at 250 tons (226.8 metric tons). R. J. J.

SEE ALSO: AERODYNAMICS, AIRCRAFT

Albatross (AL-bah-trahs) Albatrosses belong to a group of birds known as the *tube-nosed swimmers.* About sixteen species have been named. Most live only in the waters of the South Pacific.

These great birds are unequaled in their power of flight and in their wing spread. The wandering albatross has a wing spread up to 12 feet (3.66 meters). They have been known to follow ships for days, gliding along effortlessly without alighting.

Albatrosses, with their webbed feet and dense oily plumage, are especially suited for life on the sea. They seldom leave it except to rear their young on barren ocean islands.

The female lays a single egg which may require several months to hatch. The slow-growing baby is fed for five or six months before it is capable of independent flight.

The albatross may snatch greedily at refuse from ships, but most of its food consists of squid, cuttlefish, and other forms of marine life. M. D. F.

Albino (al-BYE-no) An albino is an animal with pale skin, white hair, and pink eyes. Such animals have none of the black pigment which gives color to these parts of the body. This black protects the skin from heat and light. Because their skin is not protected, albinos become sunburned very easily. They often blink and squint in the bright sunshine.

The black PIGMENT in normal skin is called *melanin.* In the albino, the cells that normally produce melanin are unable to do so. Certain reactive substances known as chromagens and ENZYMES must be present. They then must react with one another in a series of chemical processes in the proper time sequence. The albino GENE in the nucleus of each cell controls pigment formation and prevents completion of this process. When pigment is absent, the red color of the blood can be seen through the rather transparent tissues giving a pink tinge to the skin or eyes. Since no blood circulates in the hair, the hair is white.

Albino characteristics are hereditary. The albino gene is recessive. This means that parents who do not appear to have albino characteristics may have children who are albinos. Two albino parents always have albino children.

Albinism may occur in varying degrees. If the cell can make no pigment at all the individual is a true albino. Sometimes pigment is formed but in small amounts or in an incomplete form. This individual is blond in appearance. Other eye and skin colors ranging from light to very dark are found in individuals depending on the amount and kind of pigment produced in the cells. This explains why the many peoples of the world have many different skin colors.

Sometimes plants are referred to as albinos. These plants are white because they lack the characteristic plant pigments in their cells—CHLOROPHYLL, which is green; carotene and xanthophyll, which are yellow.

SEE ALSO: HEREDITY B. B. G.

A typical albino animal

F. A. Blashfield

Albumin (al-BYOO-mihn) Albumin is a simple PROTEIN common in animal and vegetable tissue. It is soluble in water and can be coagulated by heat. In man, serum albumin accounts for about 50% of the BLOOD plasma protein and is responsible for maintaining solution balance in the blood. Ovalbumin is the major protein of familiar EGG white.

Alchemy Alchemy was a combination of chemistry and magic. In ancient times and during the Middle Ages, magicians and so-called wise men sometimes worked with chemicals in trying to change one thing into another. They were often interested only in the weird effects. Those who experimented with chemical changes and effects were called alchemists. Alchemists are now felt to be unscientific, but some of their ideas and strange arts of mixing and heating led to the modern science of chemistry.

One of the persistent goals of alchemy was to change the common metals—such as lead and mercury—into "noble metals" like gold and silver. Another goal was to discover a "philosopher's stone," a material supposed to cure all diseases and make people live longer or forever. Lacking our modern knowledge of the elements and of atomic structure, the alchemists tried various mixtures, mainly by trial and error.

For centuries, medieval kings hired alchemists, hoping to gain health and wealth from their promised wonders. Such noted 13th century philosophers as Albertus Magnus and Roger Bacon supported alchemy. By the 16th century, alchemy was losing respect. Theophrastus Paracelsus (1490–1540), was one of the last well-known alchemists, and even he raised many questions about the old, useless magical methods.

Today chemical wonders can be controlled and produced and diseases cured not by the magic of alchemy, but through patient, intelligent use of systematic science. D. A. B.

SEE ALSO: ATOM, CHEMISTRY, SCIENTIFIC METHOD

Alchemists mixed chemicals mainly by trial and error

Alcohol The two best known of the many alcohols are methyl (wood) alcohol and ethyl (grain) alcohol. The various kinds have different uses, and all of them have poisonous properties. The main uses include: dissolving other chemicals, for fuel, and for making other valuable chemicals such as ETHER and flavorings.

WOOD ALCOHOL

From the careful distillation of wood, chemists get methyl alcohol (methanol). Molecularly it is the simplest of all the kinds of alcohol: CH_3OH. That is, each molecule has one carbon atom with three hydrogen atoms attached, and another hydrogen atom connected by an oxygen atom. (All the alcohols have the C-OH or carbonol group.)

Methyl alcohol is very poisonous in our bodies, causing blindness and even more severe damage to health than grain alcohol. Its uses are mainly as a modifier of ethyl alcohol, as a fuel and as an active ingredient in formaldehyde.

GRAIN OR ETHYL ALCOHOL

Almost any water solution of a sugary or starchy food can be fermented by certain ENZYMES and by YEAST cells to form ethyl alcohol. Grains are often used. Such fermented liquids may be made into beers or wines.

Molecularly, ethyl alcohol is C_2H_5OH; its boiling point is 173° F (78.3° C), its freezing point is minus (—) 170° F (-112.22° C.)

Ethyl alcohol (ethanol) has many uses. In medicine, a 70% solution of ethanol is used as an antiseptic and coagulant. In industry, ethanol is used as a solvent for perfumes, varnishes, and shellacs. Ethanol is used as a starting material for other organic compounds, such as acetic acid.

Ethanol as a beverage is substantially taxed. Methyl alcohol (methanol) is used to denature or poison it, thus insuring its legal use in industry.

Isopropyl alcohol is used as rubbing alcohol. Ethylene glycol (1,2-ethanediol) is a constituent of antifreeze. Glycerine (1,2,3-propanetriol), found in animal fats, is used in cosmetics and medicines. Alcohols are used to make esters or artificial flavors. N-amyl alcohol gives banana flavor; octyl alcohol gives orange. D. A. B. / A. J. H.

Aldebaran see Taurus

Alcoholism The complex disease in which people frequently and uncontrollably drink alcoholic beverages in excess is called alcoholism. Up to ten percent of all adult men and five percent of all adult women suffer from it. Untreated, alcoholism can result in liver damage and other medical problems and eventually death. Many social problems, including traffic accidents, violent crimes, job loss, broken families, and suicides are often related to alcoholism.

A form of ADDICTION, alcoholism can begin at any time from adolescence to old age. Sufferers who successfully combat the disease often consider themselves "recovering alcoholics" for the rest of their lives.

Little is known about the exact causes of alcoholism, but HEREDITY plays a role. Sons of alcoholic fathers are four times as likely to become alcoholics as the sons of nonalcoholic fathers, even if they are brought up outside an alcoholic home. The extent of alcoholism in various ethnic groups varies widely.

Medical treatment can include hospitalization and outpatient programs. Most approaches begin by helping the alcoholic understand the extent of the problem. Some of the best success records have been achieved by nonmedical support groups such as Alcoholics Anonymous. In 1992, University of Pennsylvania researchers noted that the drug naltrexone might act to reduce an alcoholic's craving for alcohol. J.H.

SEE ALSO: ALCOHOL, ADDICTION

Aldebaran See Taurus

Alewife Alewife belongs to the herring family. It is silvery scaled underneath with a bluish back and forked tail. Fins do not have spines. Pectoral fins are on the abdomen. A dark spot occurs behind the bony gill cover.

This fish leaves the sea to reproduce in fresh water. The 10-12 inch (25.4-30.48 centimeter) adult swims up the rivers in the spring and spawns. The young stay in fresh water until fall. When about 2-3 inches (5.08-7.62 centimeters) long they return to the sea.

Alewives often become landlocked in lakes. They have become somewhat of a pest to commercial fishermen because they clog the holes in their nets. Recently, along with the lamprey eels, they have invaded the Great Lakes. J.C.K.

SEE ALSO: HERRING, LAMPREY EEL

Alfalfa Alfalfa is an important plant fed to farm animals. Like CLOVER, it is a member of the pea family and is a source of PROTEIN for cattle. Alfalfa can be grown where many other plants cannot because its long, strong roots, grow deeply in dry soil.

Because alfalfa has nitrogen-fixing BACTERIA living in growths on its roots, it enriches the soil with nitrogen taken from the air in the soil. The plants send up fat, green shoots, 12 to 40 inches high (30.48 to 101.6 centimeters), with compound leaves.

Four-fifths of the alfalfa raised in America is used as hay. The production of alfalfa in the United States is between 50 and 65 million tons a year. J.K.K.

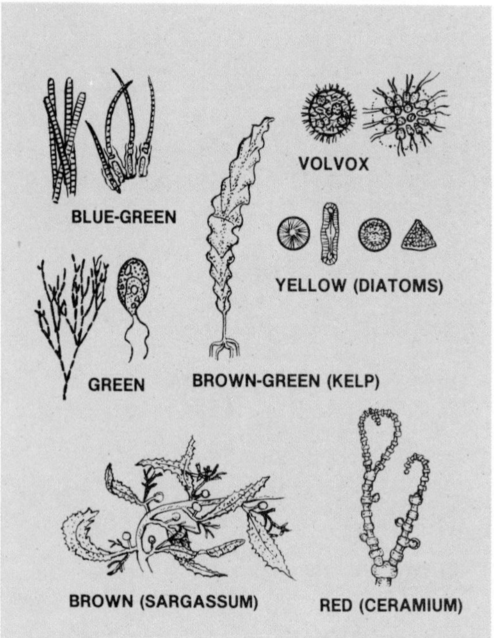

EXAMPLES OF ALGAE STRUCTURE

Algae (AL-gee) The simplest and oldest green plants belong to a group called *algae.* Common examples are pond scum and seaweed. They vary in size from plants 200 feet (60.96 meters) long to others so small they can be seen only with a microscope. Algae are classified into groups according to color—blue, green, yellow, red, or brown. They all contain CHLOROPHYLL and can make their own food. Some algae are independent one-celled plants that carry on all processes necessary for life. Many live in colonies of balls, long strands, or sheets. All lack true roots, stems, or leaves.

Algae can live in a variety of places, such as the bark of trees, fence posts, ponds, rivers, lakes or oceans. An environment with water is necessary for them to carry on reproduction. They will reproduce asexually by *fission* or by SPORE FORMATION. At times they will produce *gametes* (sex cells) which unite to form a fertilized egg called a *zygote.* This zygote germinates into a new plant under the proper conditions.

Economically, algae are important to man. The large brown-green KELPS are a source of iodine and fertilizer. Green algae are dried and pressed into cakes to serve as food for man. Several kinds of algae have a jelly-like covering used in puddings, shoe polish, agar and face creams. The substance obtained from algae for use in these various products is called *algin.* Fossil remains of the algae called DIATOMS have industrial uses.

EUGLENA, VOLVOX and other algae in the division *Euglenophyta* are classified as both plants and animals. The zoologists claim them because of their ability to move. The botanists say they are plants because they contain chlorophyll. They can also be considered as *intermediate* forms, like the ancestors of both plants and animals.

The blue-green algae (division *Cyanophyta)* are thought to be the most primitive algae. Some botanists classify blue-green algae with the BACTERIA because these groups have characteristics in common. Blue-green algae may be one-celled, joined together to form filaments, or colonial. The *chromatin* bodies (hereditary material) are not held within a nucleus but lie free within the cell. The characteristic pigments—blue and green—also are free in the protoplasm without being confined to special pigmented structures called *plastids.* As a rule, reproduction is by simple division.

The green algae (division *Chlorophyta*) derive their color from chlorophyll. In this group, as in all higher groups of algae, there is a definite nucleus and the pigments are contained in PLASTIDS. Some green algae are one-celled but others are rather highly organized into many-celled plants.

The yellow algae (division *Chrysophyta*)

Macmillan Science Company

Algae often grows in warm coastal waters.

contain large amounts of CAROTENE and XANTHOPHYLL, pigments which give them their yellow color. DIATOMS, the minute, single-celled plants with cell walls of silicon, are members of this group.

The red (division *Rhodophyta*) and brown (division *Phaeophyta*) show the highest degree of organization of all algae. They contain many specialized cells and tissues, particularly those concerned with reproduction. The brown ones live in cold oceans and include kelps and rockweeds. Some red live in warm and others in cold water. B. B. G.

SEE ALSO: PLANTS, CLASSIFICATION OF

Algebra (AL-juh-brah) Algebra is actually an extension of ARITHMETIC. It uses the same operations, the same basic laws and the same symbols as arithmetic. In fact, algebra is often known as generalized arithmetic. Algebra differs from arithmetic in that more stress is placed on the use of letters to stand for numbers, on the use of equations and inequalities in problem solving, and on the use of negative and imaginary numbers.

The word algebra comes from an Arabic word "al-jebr," which was a word in a title of a book by the Arab mathematician al-Khowarizmi in the ninth century. This word referred to certain topics dealing with equations.

Algebra uses more symbols and uses symbols more often than does arithmetic. The symbol $\neq$ means "is not equal to." One may write: $6 \neq 4$. The symbol $<$ means "is less than" and the symbol $>$ means "is greater than." For example, $7 > 3$ and $4 < 5$. Multiplication is indicated by a dot or by parentheses around the factors and no sign between the sets of parentheses. For example, -7 multiplied by $+2$ would be written $(-7)(+2)$; $3a^2$ multiplied by $2b^3$ as $3a^2 \cdot 2b^3$. Parentheses ( ), brackets [ ], braces { } , and the vinculum $\overline{\quad\quad}$ are the four commonly used symbols for grouping terms. Notice how they serve as the punctuation marks of algebra:

$$3x - \{-4 + [8x^2 - x(5 + \overline{2 - x})] - 3\}$$

ALGEBRA

BINDING NUMBER IDEAS TOGETHER

AXIOMS (ASSUMPTIONS)
THEOREMS (RULES)
ALGORITHMS (PROCEDURES)

LETTERS OR SYMBOLS REPRESENT NUMBERS OR OPERATIONS

TOGETHER THEY REPRESENT PHRASES OR SENTENCES

$6 + y$
"6 plus something (y)"

$8z = 40$
"8 times something (z) equals 40"

IF THE LETTER n IS EQUAL TO 8,
$2n = 16$
$n \div 2 = 4$
$n \cdot n = 64$

SOMETIMES THE LETTER IS COMBINED WITH NUMBERS
$5(n + 4) = 50$

AND ITS VALUE IS NOT KNOWN.

TO FIND THE VALUE OF n, USE THE DISTRIBUTIVE PROPERTY
$5(n + 4) = 5n + 20$
So, $5n + 20 = 50$

IF 50 IS 20 MORE THAN 5n,
Then $5n = 30$
And $n = 6$

NOW CHECK: DOES $5(n + 4) = 50$ IF $n = 6$?
$5(6 + 4) = 5(10) = 50$

NOW TRY THIS PROBLEM:
$6m - 10 = 8$
$m = ?$

Elementary algebra usually begins with a study of the properties of the natural numbers, followed by the properties of the integers, the rational numbers, and the irrational numbers. The natural numbers are the numbers used in counting. They are represented by the symbols 1,2,3, · · · (the three dots indicate an unending succession of symbols). If a + sign is put in front of each natural number, the set of symbols is known as the *positive integers.* If +2 may be compared with a reading on a thermometer of two degrees above zero, then −2 would be considered as two degrees below zero. If each of the positive integers had its + sign replaced by a − sign, the set of symbols so created would be called the *negative integers.* The positive integers, the negative integers and zero form the set of the integers. Note that the sum of +3 and −3 is zero; the sum of +8 and −8 is zero; the sum of $+n$ and $-n$ (n is an integer) is zero. +2 is said to be the opposite of −2. For this reason the integers are thought of as directed numbers.

A *rational number* is one which can be expressed as the quotient of an integer and a nonzero integer. The proper and improper fractions of arithmetic are rational numbers. Any periodic decimal is also a rational number. For example, .272727 . . . is a rational number because it is equal to $\frac{3}{11}$ 2.3060606 . . . is a rational number because it is equal to $\frac{761}{330}$. Irrational numbers can not be written as the ratio of an integer to a nonzero integer, nor as periodic decimals. The set of the rational numbers together with the set of the irrational numbers comprise the *real numbers.* This is why rational numbers are often defined as numbers which can be expressed as decimals. Properties that hold true for the integers and the rationals in general hold true for the real numbers.

Exponents play a big role in the study of algebra. The symbol x^n represents $x \cdot x \cdot x \cdots x$, where the number x is taken n times as a factor; n is called the exponent and x the base. Here n can only stand for a positive integer. For example, $2^5 = 2 \cdot 2 \cdot 2 \cdot 2 \cdot 2 = 32$, and $4^3 = 4 \cdot 4 \cdot 4 = 64$.

Symbols like 2, π, $\div$, $\frac{5}{2}$ stand for explicit numbers because the relationship between the symbols and the numbers is definitely stated. In the formula $V = e^3$, V represents the volume of a cube and e its edge. Letters so used are *literal numbers* because they represent real numbers. If a symbol stands for any number in a specified set of numbers that symbol is called a *variable* and the set of numbers is called the *domain* of the variable.

An algebraic expression is composed of symbols which are combined by one or more of the operations of algebra. An algebraic expression represents a number. A term is composed of a single symbol, or of symbols, combined by any of the operations of algebra except addition or subtraction. Any factor of a term is a *coefficient* of the remaining factor, or of the product of the remaining factors of the term. For example, in the term $2xy^2$, 2 is the coefficient of xy^2, x is the coefficient of $2y^2$, y^2 is the coefficient of $2x$. An expression of one term is a *monomial;* of two terms, a *binomial;* of two or more terms, is a *multinomial.*

Algebra is used to solve many problems. Once one knows how to represent problems algebraically and how to handle algebraic symbols and operations, many problems can be solved. Consider this problem:

A strip 4 meters wide was cut from one side of a square, and a strip 2 meters wide was cut from an adjacent side. The area of the rectangle that remained was 24 square meters. What was the area of the original square?

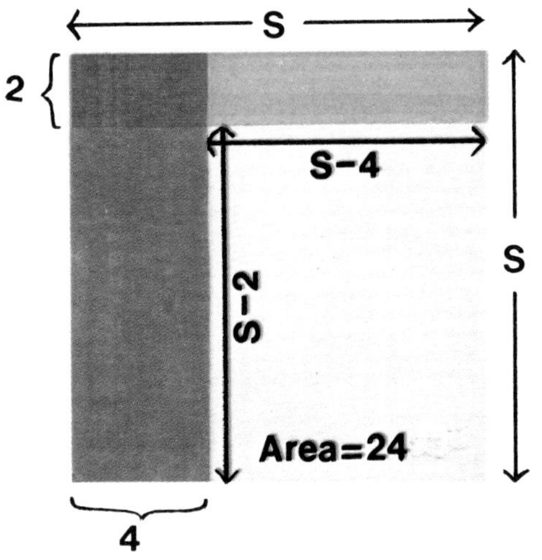

Let s be the length of the side of the square.

Then, $s-2$ and $s-4$ are the dimensions of the rectangle.

Since the area of the rectangle is 24,

$(s-2)(s-4) = 24\}$ (express the problem algebraically)

$$\left.\begin{aligned} s^2-6s+8 &= 24 \\ s^2-6s-16 &= 0 \\ (s-8)(s+2) &= 0 \end{aligned}\right\} \text{(using algebraic procedures)}$$

Using the property of 0, $(s-8) = 0$ or $(s+2) = 0$, so $s = 8$ or $s = -2$. Since the side cannot be a negative length, the length of the side must be 8 meters. Thus, the area of the original square was $8 \cdot 8$ or 64 square meters.

Alimentary canal The alimentary canal is a continuous tube from the anterior opening to the posterior opening in many animals. In it, most processes of digestion take place.

SEE: ANIMAL, DIGESTIVE SYSTEM

Alkali see Acids and bases

Alkali deposits Alkali deposits are beds of salts left when water evaporates from marshes and lakes in dry regions. These salt deposits are found at Great Salt Lake in Utah, at Lake Eyre in southern Australia, and on the shores of the Aral, Caspian, and Dead seas.

In desert areas, water drains into low, flat basins where sun and wind evaporate it. Mineral salts and alkalies, present in the mud and water, do not evaporate, and when completely dried, they form crusts of salt crystals. Sometimes these are very white. In less dry regions alkali materials wash out of the soil and are carried to the ocean by the rivers.

Some plants grow in soil that is alkaline, but most agricultural plants will grow best in soil that is slightly acid. If the soil contains a great deal of salts and alkalies or is extremely acid, plants will not grow at all. It is difficult to correct alkaline soils in a short period of time. Acid soils can be corrected in a relatively short period of time by applying limestone. A. P. M.

SEE ALSO: ACIDS AND BASES, SALTS

Allegheny Mountains see North America

Allergy The body is normally protected from many harmful diseases by refusing to allow the living substances or products of another kind of animal or plant to remain within it. As soon as any foreign material enters the body, the tissues that are invaded send out a call for protection. These tissues swell and become reddened as the

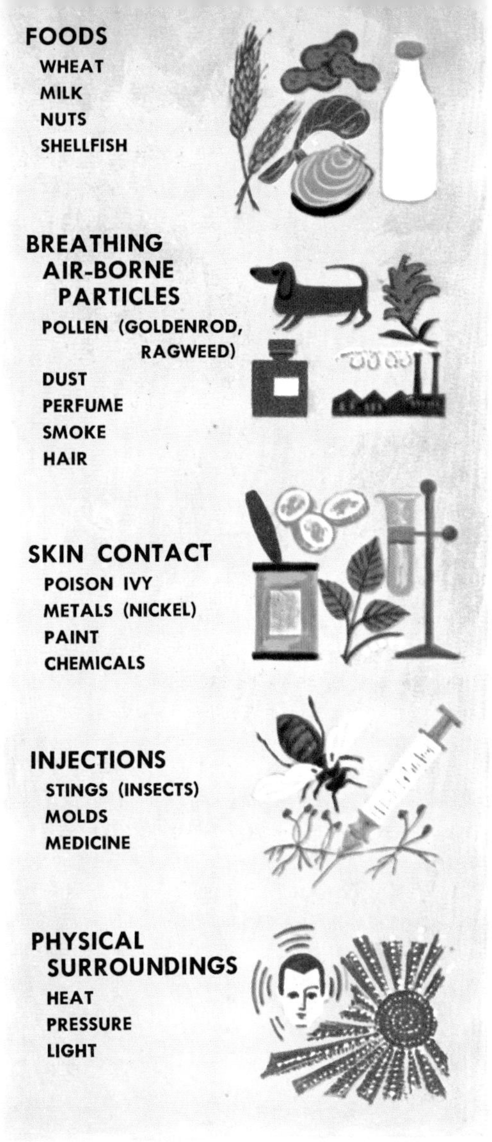

Many things can cause allergic reactions.

blood supply increases in an attempt to fight and win over the enemy. However, when the body has a reaction that is too strong for the amount of danger involved, this becomes an *allergic reaction.*

One can think of allergic reactions as unfavorable reactions of the body to a foreign substance or *allergen* following at least one contact. Anything that causes a body reaction is called an *antigen.* When antigens cause an extreme reaction they are then called *allergens.* This only happens after the body has been exposed to the particular allergen at least one time. For example, nobody reacts to poison ivy the first time he touches it. But after that the reaction varies with the individual's sensitivity.

There are two main types of allergic reactions. 1. *Immediate hypersensitivity* is associated with formation of serum antibody (a globulin protein that attaches to the antigen to try to make it chemically inactive). 2. *Delayed hypersensitivity* which is unassociated with serum antibody. Immediate hypersensitivity reactions include ASTHMA and HAY FEVER. These are thought to be somehow related to the amount of antigen-antibody combination circulating in the bloodstream. Too much antigen for the body to handle will cause an allergic reaction. Reactions to bacterial toxins (poisons) and contact dermatitis (skin rash from poison ivy or metals) are thought to be delayed hypersensitivity reactions. *Histamines* are formed in allergic reactions. These add to distress by causing dilation of blood vessels and swelling of nearby tissues.

The symptoms of HAY FEVER (running nose and itching watery eyes), ASTHMA, skin rashes, HIVES, stomach and intestinal upset are caused by inflammation of the tissues of various parts of the body where the allergic reaction is taking place.

The breathing in of POLLEN, fungus spores, vegetable or animal oils, or dust is a common cause of respiratory allergy. Wheat, eggs, milk, nuts, chocolate, and strawberries are common food allergens.

Allergic reactions are treated by avoiding the allergen, taking anti-histamine drugs, hyposensitizing (usually with injections) by gradual increased exposure to the allergen, and taking cortisone (rarely) to decrease inflammation, or using it as an ointment on affected skin areas. E. S. S.

SEE ALSO: ANTIBODY

Alligator The alligator is a REPTILE that lives in and out of water. It is a cold-blooded animal. Baby alligators are hatched from eggs. The alligator is known for its big jaws and teeth. It will eat almost any kind of land or water animal up to the size of a deer. Baby alligators eat water insects. As they grow they learn to eat fish, frogs, birds, and other warm- and cold-blooded animals. Alligators grow from a few inches (centimeters) at birth to be about 10 feet (3.05 meters).

Courtesy Society For Visual Education, Inc.

Sleepy alligators dozing in the sun

Alligators live in the southern coastal areas of the United States and along the Yangtze River in China. They are members of the CROCODILE family. The alligator's snout is broader than the crocodile's.

In April or May the female alligator makes a large mud nest of grass, twigs, and leaves. When it is completed, she deposits from 20 to 70 eggs and completely covers them with plants. The heat of the sun and the decomposition of the warm moist nest aid in the incubation of the eggs, which takes 2 to 2½ months.

Today the use of alligator skin for leather is greatly reduced. Hides cannot be shipped out of states where these endangered species live. Concerned people are fighting to save these reptiles. M. E. C.

Allosaurus see Dinosaur

Alloy An alloy is a mixture of two or more metals. Brass is an alloy of copper and zinc. Bronze is tin mixed with copper. The combination of metals is made possible by heating them until they become liquid. A *true* alloy is formed if the metals remain evenly mixed when they are cooled and become a solid.

Alloys are made because they have more suitable uses than do the simple metals alone. For example, pure copper is much softer than its copper-tin alloy, bronze.

Practically all metals in manufactured items are alloys. STEEL is composed of carbon, iron, and certain other substances. Aluminum ware contains aluminum, manganese, silicon, and magnesium. Among the other alloys in common use are those that contain nickel, lead, and titanium. Ferrous alloys use iron as their main element, and non-ferrous alloys are made of other metals.

Each type of alloying element produces a certain effect on the total mass of METAL.

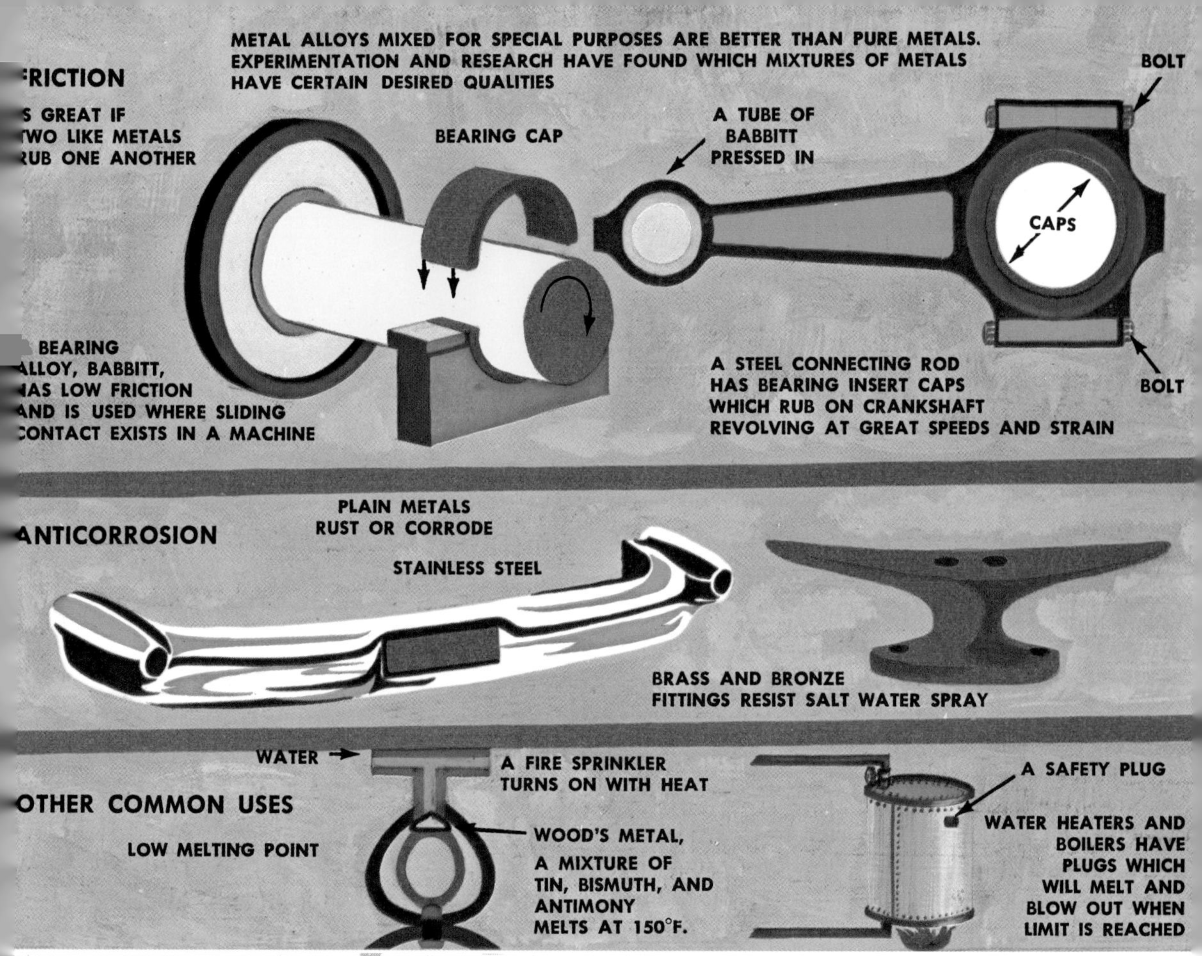
METAL ALLOYS MIXED FOR SPECIAL PURPOSES ARE BETTER THAN PURE METALS. EXPERIMENTATION AND RESEARCH HAVE FOUND WHICH MIXTURES OF METALS HAVE CERTAIN DESIRED QUALITIES
FRICTION
S GREAT IF
WO LIKE METALS
UB ONE ANOTHER
BEARING CAP
A TUBE OF BABBITT PRESSED IN
BOLT
CAPS
BEARING
ALLOY, BABBITT,
AS LOW FRICTION
AND IS USED WHERE SLIDING
ONTACT EXISTS IN A MACHINE
A STEEL CONNECTING ROD HAS BEARING INSERT CAPS WHICH RUB ON CRANKSHAFT REVOLVING AT GREAT SPEEDS AND STRAIN
BOLT
ANTICORROSION
PLAIN METALS RUST OR CORRODE
STAINLESS STEEL
BRASS AND BRONZE FITTINGS RESIST SALT WATER SPRAY
OTHER COMMON USES
LOW MELTING POINT
WATER →
A FIRE SPRINKLER TURNS ON WITH HEAT
WOOD'S METAL, A MIXTURE OF TIN, BISMUTH, AND ANTIMONY MELTS AT 150°F.
A SAFETY PLUG
WATER HEATERS AND BOILERS HAVE PLUGS WHICH WILL MELT AND BLOW OUT WHEN LIMIT IS REACHED

SOME IMPORTANT ALLOYS	PERCENTAGES OF ELEMENTS	MAIN PROPERTIES; USES
COIN ALLOY WHITE METAL	Copper 75%, nickel 25%	Durable; U.S. 5¢, 10¢, 25¢ coins
COPPER COIN ALLOY	Copper 95%, zinc & tin 5%	Durable, cheap; U.S. 1¢ piece
BABBITT BEARING METAL	Tin 91%, antimony 4½% copper 4½%	Friction resistant; for lining machine bearings
ALLOY "SILVER"	Copper 60%, nickel 15%, zinc 25%, no silver	Hard, corrosion resistant, silvery color; tableware, keys, medical instruments
YELLOW BRASS*	Copper 66%, zinc 34%	Gold color, moderately hard, non-corrosive; ornaments, shell casings
DURALUMIN	Aluminum 90%, manganese 5½% copper 4%, magnesium ½%	Light, strong; airplane structures
WOOD'S METAL	Lead 25%, bismuth 50%, tin 12½%, cadmium 12½%	Low melting point; fire alarms, sprinklers, fuses
STAINLESS STEEL*	Iron 50%, nickel 24%, chromium 20%, molybdenum 3%, silicon 3%	Acid and alkali resistant, fairly hard; tableware, instruments
NICHROME*	Nickel 60%, iron 25%, chromium 15%	High melting point, low electrical conductivity; electric heaters, toasters

*A number of alloys are known under the same name

The stainless properties in steel are produced by adding chromium, nickel, and molybdenum. Stainless steel also has greater strength. Tungsten increases resistance to abrasion and gives greater hardness at high temperatures. Phosphorus makes low-carbon steel stronger and easier to work. Vanadium and aluminum harden metal and give it a smooth, solid crystal structure. Lead and zinc have low melting points and make it easier to machine, or to cast their alloys.

The most common use of lead alloy is the making of the ELECTRODES of storage batteries. Since zinc alloys aid in chrome and nickel plating, they are important in the manufacture of automobiles. D. E. Z.

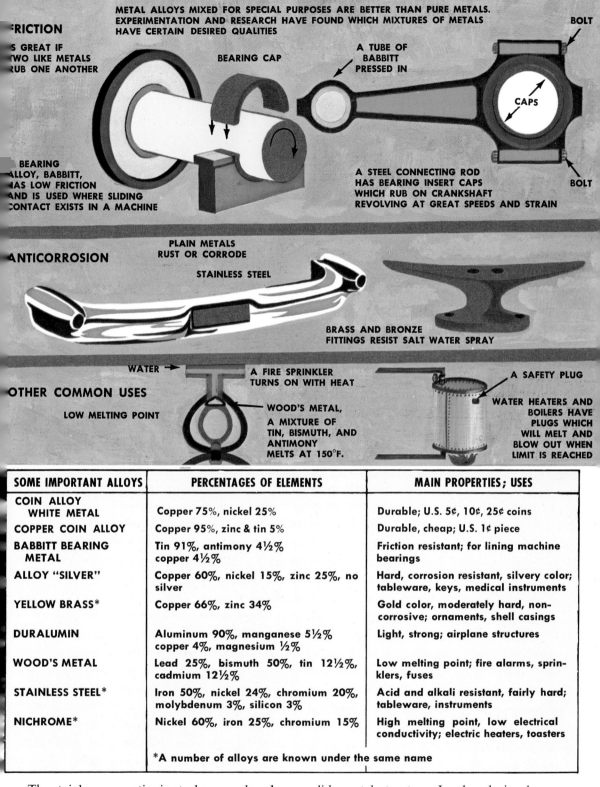

The allspice tree gives man a familiar food seasoning

The flowering almond is one of the most beautiful trees

Allspice Allspice comes from a berry on the pimento tree which grows in the West Indies and Central America. It is called allspice because the taste and smell of the berry is like cinnamon, cloves and nutmeg together. The allspice flavor is used in foods and medicines.

The berry from the pimento, or allspice tree, as it is often called, is small, sweet and juicy when ripe. But it must be picked and dried while still green to obtain the allspice flavor. The name of the tree—*pimento*—comes from the Spanish word meaning "peppercorn." Whole allspice is used for seasoning in pickles, meats, gravies, sausages and cheese. Ground allspice is used in cakes, cookies, pies, soups, salads and vegetables.

Alluvial soil see Soil types

Almond The almond is a flowering tree belonging to the rose family. It is related to roses and such fruit trees as apple, peach, plum and apricot. Almond trees are grown in warm climates, as in California or along the Mediterranean. The so-called "nut" of the *sweet* almond is eaten, used in cooking and gives almond oil when pressed. It is not a nut but the seed of a fruit.

Hydrocyanic acid in the seed of the *bitter* almond makes it too bitter to eat. Bitter or sweet, the almond fruit is a drupe with a leathery wall developing from the outer parts of the wall of the flower ovary. When almonds are harvested, the leathery portion is removed, making the former inner part of the ovarian wall the "shell" of the "nut." J. C. K.

SEE ALSO: NUTS

Alpaca (al-PACK-uh) The alpaca is a large, woolly animal. It looks like a sheep with the head of a camel. It lives only high in the Andes Mountains of South America. The natives of the mountain countries take care of them in flocks. The WOOL of the alpaca is used to make fine and soft cloth.

The feet of the alpaca are split and have hooked spurs which help them live on the steep mountain-sides. The wool is often allowed to grow for several years before it is sheared, so the hair grows to be very long. Fabric made from such wool is very cool, light and durable.

The alpaca is one of four South American mammals which is traced back directly to the CAMEL of pre-historic times. So the camel and the LLAMA are related to it. M. E. C.

The alpaca is related to the llama and camel.

San Diego Zoo

Alpha Alpha is the first letter of the Greek alphabet. It is sometimes used to name the brightest star of a group called a CONSTELLATION.

"Alpha Orionis" means the brightest star of the constellation Orion. In order of their brightness, the stars of the constellation are named for other letters of the Greek alphabet. Astronomers use numbers after they have exhausted the letters of the alphabet.

Occasionally, astronomers follow the shape of the constellation in giving the first names to stars instead of the order of brightness. The stars of the Big Dipper are named this way. C. L. K.

Alpha rays see Radiation; Ray, alpha

Alps Mountains see Europe

Altair see Aquila

Alternating current see Electricity

Alternation of generations In plants, an egg and sperm-forming plant alternates, or takes turns with, a plant which forms spores. This life cycle is called alternation of generations. There is first an egg-and-sperm-forming plant followed by a spore-forming, and then by an egg-and-sperm-forming plant again.

Each kind or species of plant has the number of CHROMOSOMES (hereditary factors) in its nucleus that is constant for that kind of plant. For example, Polypodium, a common fern, has eight chromosomes. The nuclei of the spore-bearing plant, called a *sporophyte* (fern plant), have eight chromosomes. This is the full number of chromosomes for that species. The sporophyte produces cells called *spores*. Each spore can become an egg- and sperm-forming plant known as a *gametophyte*. When the spores are formed, the number of chromosomes are reduced by half. Therefore, the spores and gametophytes into which they develop have four chromosomes in their nuclei. The gametophytes produce egg and sperm cells. The nuclei of both eggs and sperm have four chromosomes. When an egg and sperm cell unite, the new cell formed is called a ZYGOTE. It has eight chromosomes. The zygote develops into a new sporophyte plant and the cycle starts over again.

In seed plants, the trees, shrubs, and flowering herbs are sporophytes. The gametophytes have been reduced during evolution to the short span between halving the chromosome number and fertilization.

In animals, the alternation between hydroid and medusa forms in coelenterates is sometimes called alternation of generations. This alternation, however, is between the sexually immature hydroid and the sexually mature medusa without any change in chromosome number.

There are really two aspects to alternation of generations: *morphological* alternation—change in types of structure (as in plants) and *cytological* alternation—change in chromosome number (as in both plants and animals). B. B. G.

SEE ALSO: HEREDITY, MITOSIS AND MEIOSIS

Alternation of host see Parasites

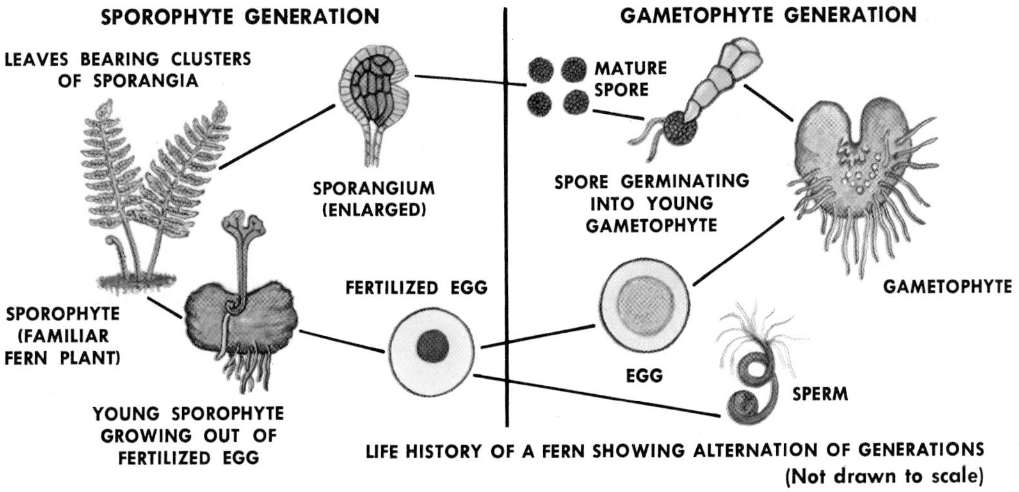

LIFE HISTORY OF A FERN SHOWING ALTERNATION OF GENERATIONS
(Not drawn to scale)

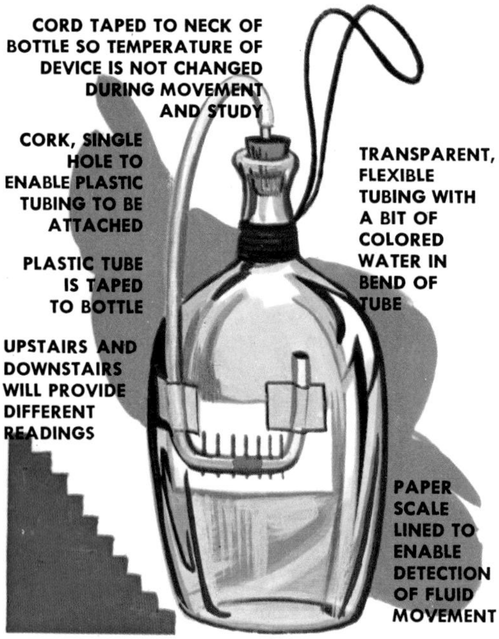

Principle of an aircraft altimeter

Altimeter (al-TIM-uh-ter) The altimeter is an instrument to measure altitude above the earth. All aircraft are required to have altimeters. The *barometric altimeter* measures the height above sea level. The *radio altimeter* is an electronic device which measures actual height of the aircraft, over the surface below it.

The sensitive altimeter used in aircraft is essentially an aneroid barometer. It reacts to changes in atmospheric pressure to give a calibrated reading in feet instead of inches of mercury. The instrument is enclosed in an airtight case connected to the static side of the aircraft Pitot tube, located on the leading edge of the wing.

It is necessary for the pilot to initially adjust the barometric scale of the instrument before each flight. This setting varies daily as the atmospheric pressure at any point on the earth's surface is constantly changing. Although air pressure generally decreases with altitude, it is necessary for the pilot in flight to frequently monitor and adjust his altimeter setting. The pilot receives this information by radio from flight service stations along his route.

The radio altimeter is basically a simplified radar transceiver. Electronic signals are sent to the ground below the aircraft and are reflected back to the receiver. An electronic timing device translates the time lapse between the signal transmission and reception into the actual feet of altitude above the ground. There are obvious advantages of having this direct reading. This electronic equipment is quite expensive and is usually found in military and larger commercial aircraft.

In flight, altitude control is vital to proper air traffic control, especially during instrument flight in poor weather. R. J. J.

SEE ALSO: ATMOSPHERE, SEA LEVEL, SPACE

Altitude The height of an object (a boy in a tree) above a level (the ground under the tree) is its *altitude.* Sea level is often used by scientists to figure altitudes. The height of an object above sea level is given in feet, miles, meters, and kilometers. The altitudes of mountains are spoken of as *elevations.* Mt. Everest, the highest mountain on earth, has an elevation of 29,028 feet (8,847.73 meters).

Maps show altitudes by using contour lines. The lines come closer together to show a land form becoming steeper. Aeronautical charts use lines and mark highest elevation by dots and numbers of feet. Instruments such as barometric ALTIMETER record the altitudes of objects above the ground.

The atmosphere of the earth has different characteristics at different altitudes. In the troposphere, the lowest layer of the atmosphere, temperatures decrease with an increase of altitude. The rate of this decrease is 3½°F. for each 1,000 feet (1.1°C for each 304.8 meters) of altitude. This is called the *normal lapse rate* and is caused by the expansion of the air. E. M. N.

SEE ALSO: ATMOSPHERE, SEA LEVEL, SPACE

Alto-cumulus see Clouds

Alto-stratus see Clouds

Alum Alum refers to any of several SALTS of aluminum. One common alum is *potash alum.* The alums have many uses; among them are the PURIFICATION of water and the sizing of paper.

Alumina see Aluminum, Gem, Ruby

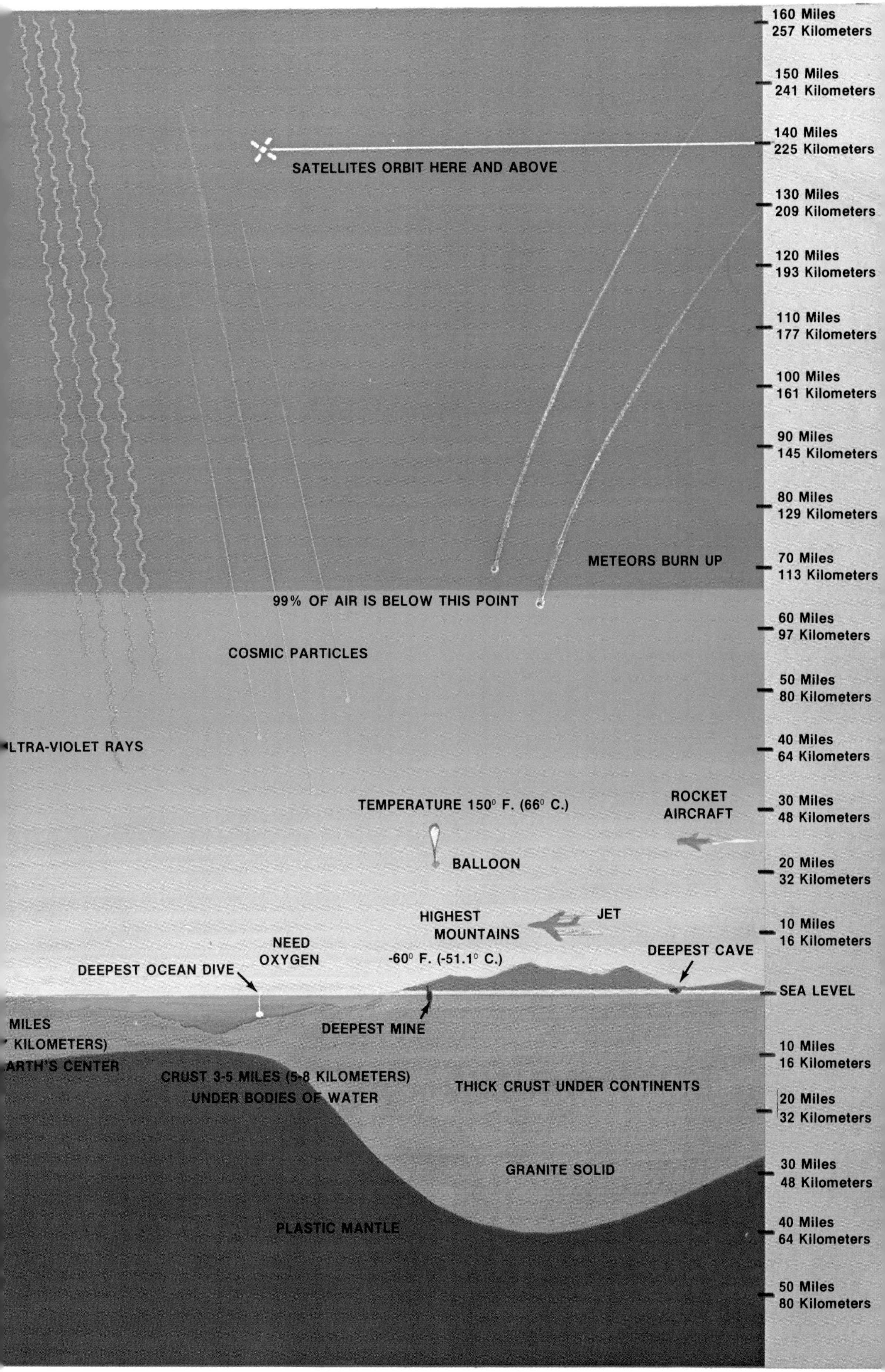

160 Miles
257 Kilometers
150 Miles
241 Kilometers
140 Miles
225 Kilometers
SATELLITES ORBIT HERE AND ABOVE
130 Miles
209 Kilometers
120 Miles
193 Kilometers
110 Miles
177 Kilometers
100 Miles
161 Kilometers
90 Miles
145 Kilometers
80 Miles
129 Kilometers
METEORS BURN UP
70 Miles
113 Kilometers
99% OF AIR IS BELOW THIS POINT
60 Miles
97 Kilometers
COSMIC PARTICLES
50 Miles
80 Kilometers
LTRA-VIOLET RAYS
40 Miles
64 Kilometers
TEMPERATURE 150° F. (66° C.)
ROCKET AIRCRAFT
30 Miles
48 Kilometers
BALLOON
20 Miles
32 Kilometers
HIGHEST MOUNTAINS
JET
10 Miles
16 Kilometers
NEED OXYGEN
-60° F. (-51.1° C.)
DEEPEST CAVE
DEEPEST OCEAN DIVE
SEA LEVEL
DEEPEST MINE
MILES
KILOMETERS)
ARTH'S CENTER
10 Miles
16 Kilometers
CRUST 3-5 MILES (5-8 KILOMETERS) UNDER BODIES OF WATER
THICK CRUST UNDER CONTINENTS
20 Miles
32 Kilometers
GRANITE SOLID
30 Miles
48 Kilometers
PLASTIC MANTLE
40 Miles
64 Kilometers
50 Miles
80 Kilometers

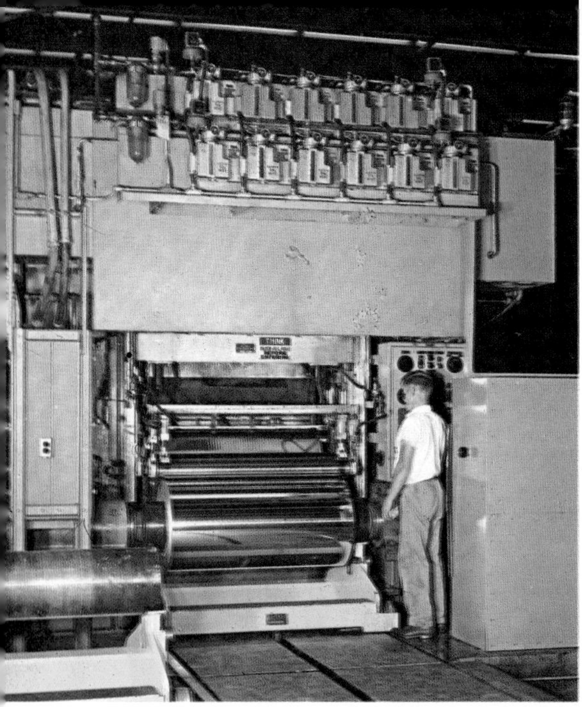

Courtesy ALCOA

Because of its strength and light weight, aluminum is used in many ways. The rolling mill above is making aluminum foil less than 6/1000 of an inch thick. Many of the sizes and shapes of aluminum foil (below) are used as electrical windings with a good conductivity.

Aluminum Aluminum is a bluish silver-white element known for its strength and light weight. After oxygen and silicon, aluminum is the most abundant element in the earth's crust. Although aluminum makes up 8% of the earth's crust, it is found only in combination with other elements. It can be easily forged, rolled, or stretched into sheets, rods, or wire. When it is mixed with other metals, it forms ALLOYS of great strength and light weight.

Aluminum weighs two and seven-tenths times as much as water or a little more than one-third as much as iron. It is a metal that strongly resists corrosion by forming a protective coating of white oxide. It is very *malleable* and fairly *ductile.* Although aluminum is very abundant in the earth's crust, the element's strong affinity for oxygen prohibits its natural occurence in the metallic state. Aluminum has a widespread distribution and is present in most rock-forming minerals. It is found most frequently in clays and other mineral compounds. Large supplies of BAUXITE, the ore from which aluminum is most cheaply extracted, are located in Arkansas, Central America, the Caribbean Islands, and most tropical climates, although large deposits are found in Russia. CORUNDUM and gibbsite are two other common mineral occurences of aluminum.

Aluminum is used in the construction of buildings, airplanes, toys, trucks, railroad cars, electric cables—its uses are numerous. It can be hammered into a thin foil which is useful in the wrapping, processing, and storing of foods, chewing gum, and cigarettes. Most cooking utensils are made of this metal.

Aluminum was discovered in 1807. The German chemist WÖHLER was the first to obtain the pure metal form of aluminum in 1827, although OERSTED probably isolated an impure form in 1825. The method of cheaply providing aluminum metal by ELECTROLYSIS of pure alumina, Al_2O_3, dissolved in cryolite, Na_3AlF_6, was discovered independently by an American, Charles HALL, and a French chemist, Paul HEROULT, in 1886.

The chemical symbol for aluminum is Al. Its atomic number is 13. Its atomic weight is 26.9815 (26.98, O = 16). Its specific gravity is close to 2.8. P.P.S.

SEE ALSO: ATOM, ELECTROLYSIS, ELEMENTS

Alzheimer's disease (ALZ-hy-merz) A condition in which a person loses a number of mental skills over varying periods of time may be the result of Alzheimer's disease. The cause is not known. At present, there is no cure or encouraging treatment.

Alzheimer's disease (AD) usually attacks mature and elderly people. Sufferers generally show a significant loss of memory. In some cases, the disease seems to progress no further. Often, however, mental abilities continue to weaken over a period of months or years. As the condition worsens, patients find it increasingly difficult to take care of even their most basic needs. Death usually comes within ten years of the onset of the disease.

A person whose family has a history of AD is more likely to eventually suffer from it. AD seems to act by damaging or destroying nerve cells in the BRAIN, primarily in the areas that control thought. In 1992, researchers in Washington, D.C., announced that they had discovered evidence of a genetic defect that seemed to cause an especially severe form of AD. J.H.

SEE ALSO: BRAIN, CEREBRUM, HEREDITY

Amaryllis (am-ah-RIL-is) Amaryllis is an unusually showy house plant which grows from a large bulb. It does not need full sun. Long narrow leaves grow in spring and then wither. The beautiful red, purple, pink or striped blooms rise on a tall sturdy stem. Later more leaves appear.

Amaryllis

The snowdrop, tuberose, narcissus and daffodil, which grow in gardens and in flower pots, all belong to the amaryllis family.

The bloodflower, a member of the amaryllis family, grows in South Africa. Its bulb is poisonous. The Hottentots, a South African tribe of people, use the juice to poison arrowheads. The belladonna lily, one of the amaryllis family, is used in medicine.

The best amaryllis bulbs are about the size of a teacup. The bulb should be set in a small flower pot of soil in the fall, with a bit of the bulb showing above the soil. They should be kept in a cool dark spot. P. G. B.

Amateur radio see Radio

Amazon River see South America

Amber When the oily sap of ancient cone-bearing trees was buried and hardened for ages in the earth, it formed amber. The best grades of amber are a clear, brownish yellow.

Amber is thus a fossilized RESIN. It is found in lumps lying beneath sand beds of the Oligocene epoch of ten million years ago. Some amber contains preserved insects that were caught in the sticky sap.

The largest deposits of amber occur on the southeast Baltic coast. Kalaningrad, Russia (old Koenigsberg), is the chief city of modern trade in amber. Deposits also occur in Australia, Burma, Greenland, Sicily, the United States, and the West Indies.

Amber is used to make jewelry, pipe mouthpieces, and combs. Poor grades are used in varnish.

The early Phoenicians and Greeks knew about Baltic and Sicilian amber. The Greek Thales noted how amber (called *electron* in Greek), when rubbed, attracted bits of straw: but it took over a thousand years for men to realize that this action was what is now called *static electricity*. D. A. B.

Ambergris see Whale

Amber is resin from evergreen trees that has hardened for millions of years

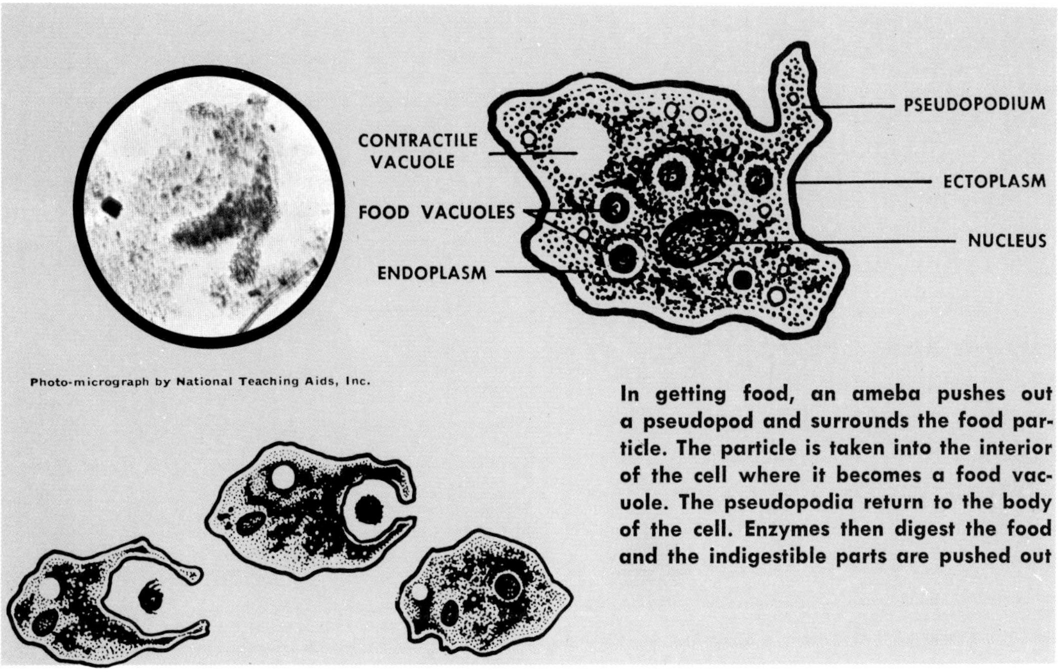

Photo-micrograph by National Teaching Aids, Inc.

In getting food, an ameba pushes out a pseudopod and surrounds the food particle. The particle is taken into the interior of the cell where it becomes a food vacuole. The pseudopodia return to the body of the cell. Enzymes then digest the food and the indigestible parts are pushed out

Ameba (uh-MEE-buh) The ameba is one of the tiniest and simplest animals. Most ameba can only be seen through a MICROSCOPE. Only one kind can be seen with the naked eye. All of its living parts are within one cell. The part of the cell which controls all of the activities of the cell (the way the brain controls man's activities) is the *nucleus.*

When the cell grows to a certain size, it divides to form two cells by simple cell division. This kind of reproduction by cell division is called *binary fission*

Possibly the ameba was one of the earliest forms of life to appear on the earth. Close relatives with shells have left a long fossil record. The group to which amebae belong is named the PROTOZOA. These animals have lived in the waters of the earth for hundreds of millions of years without much change.

The ameba moves in an interesting way. The protoplasm, or stuff of which the cell is made, is liquid in the central part of the cell, but is rather solid at the edges of the cell. The whole cell is contained within a cell membrane. The solid protoplasm gives way. Then the liquid protoplasm flows out and forms a foot-like sac called a *pseudopod* (meaning false-foot). If a solid surface is in contact with the pseudopod, the rest of the protoplasm of the cell flows into this pseudopod, and in this way the ameba moves along. If there is no solid surface in contact, the pseudopod is withdrawn and a new pseudopod breaks through at another place along the cell membrane. New pseudopodia are always being extended or withdrawn.

Not only does the ameba move along a surface by this type of locomotion, called *ameboid motion,* but it obtains its foods in the same way. If the solid particle the ameba touches is small enough to be engulfed as food, pseudopodia extend themselves along and around it until the particle is drawn into the interior of the cell. Digestion of the food then takes place within the cell. When excess fluids accumulate as wastes, they are discharged from the cell body by means of a structure called a *contractile vacuole.*

Ameboid-type cells are also found within larger organisms. White BLOOD cells (leucocytes) are ameboid and can destroy bacteria in the blood stream or in other tissues by the same engulfing action of the pseudopodia. Other amebas can cause diseases such as amebic dysentery. B. B. G.

SEE ALSO: DIGESTIVE SYSTEM

Amebic dysentery see Dysentery

Ameboid movement Ameboid movement is the manner in which cells, typically the AMEBA, move from place to place. As part of the cellular protoplasm flows in one direction, the remaining material follows.
SEE: BLOOD

Americium (Am-er-EE-see-um) Americium, element No. 95, is a man-made element. It was first discovered by Dr. Glenn T. Seaborg, R.A. James, L.O. Morgan, and A. Ghiorso in 1944. Americium was named after the Americas, as its rare earth "sister", Europium, was named after Europe.

Americium was first made by adding two neutrons to plutonium-239. The plutonium gives off a beta particle leaving Americium-241. Americium is the starting material for preparing heavier atoms. Americium-241 is bombarded by an alpha particle to produce Berkleum-243. Americium has 13 radioactive isotopes with atomic mass between 237 and 247 and half lives from 20 minutes to 7,073 years. A. J. H.
SEE ALSO: ATOM, ELEMENTS PERIODIC TABLE, NUCLEAR SCIENCE

Amethyst (AM-uh-thist) The amethyst is a mineral used in jewelry. It is usually violet or purple. Amethyst is really a semiprecious type of QUARTZ colored by traces of manganese or iron. When it is heated, it turns to a beautiful yellow or a light brown. Purple amethyst is used most often in jewelry.

As a form of quartz, amethyst mineral has a formula of SiO_2. Its hardness is 7.

Today, Russia produces many amethysts. They were known by ancient Greeks who gave the stone the name *amethystos*. They thought that any liquor drunk from a container made of it would not be intoxicating. D. E. Z.
SEE ALSO: GEM, MINERAL, ROCKS

Amino acid (uh-MEE-no) Amino acids are the chemical building blocks of PROTEINS. Proteins are a necessary part of protoplasm, which is the living substance found in plants and animals. Plants make amino acids within their cells. Animals are able to make some amino acids but have to take in others by eating protein food.

All amino acids contain nitrogen, carbon, oxygen, and hydrogen. Some also contain sulfur. Amino acids are so named because these elements are combined into molecules that have at least one basic amino group (NH_2) and at least one organic acid group (COOH). Various combinations of amino acids make up proteins. Genes on the chromosomes code (have the "blueprint" for) the order of amino acids in the proteins making up an individual plant or animal. Closely related plants or animals have many kinds of proteins in common. Their individual differences depend upon genes which code for combinations of amino acids unique to an individual plant or animal.

Some amino acids are called essential because they must be supplied in food. Nonessential amino acids are those which can be synthesized in the body. B. B. G.
SEE ALSO: DIGESTIVE SYSTEM, METABOLISM, ORGANIC COMPOUNDS

Large amethyst crystals are cut into semiprecious stones

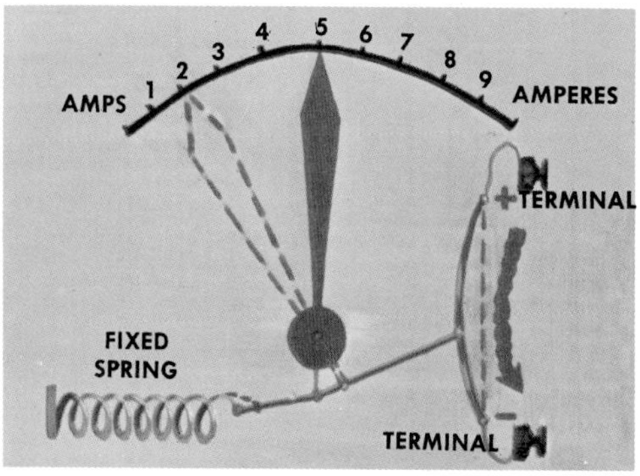

In a "hot wire" ammeter, a current moves through the wire which heats and expands. A taut spring moves the indicator as the wire expands

Ammeter (AM-mee-ter) An ammeter is a sensitive electrical instrument which measures the amount of an electrical current (amperes) flowing through an electrical circuit. The word ammeter is a contraction of the two words "AMPERE" (amount of a current) and "meter" (measuring instrument).

The operation of a common ammeter is based on magnetic attraction and repulsion. The movable part of an ammeter is a small coil of wire wound around a soft iron core and suspended on jewel bearings between the poles of a permanent MAGNET. The coil rotates against two spiral springs that retard the swing of the coil and also serve to carry the current into and away from the coil. When a current flows through the coil, a magnetic field is created within the coil which is perpendicular to that of the fixed magnet. The coil turns until its magnetic field is parallel to that of the permanent magnet. The pointer attached to the coil indicates the amount of current flowing through the coil. Most ammeters are arranged so that the amount of *deflection* (movement of the pointer) is proportional to the amount of current.

Ammeters need to operate on as low internal RESISTANCE as possible. For this reason a low resistance circuit called a *shunt* is connected in parallel with the terminals of the moving coil. An ammeter is always connected in series in the circuit in which the current is to be measured. It should never be placed in a circuit in which the current exceeds the built-in capacity of the meter.

SEE ALSO: GALVANOMETER I. K. F.

Ammonia (uh-MOAN-yuh) Ammonia is a chemical compound of nitrogen and hydrogen. Ammonia can be obtained by two processes—1) by distilling coal into coke and coal gas, 2) by combining hydrogen and nitrogen with a CATALYST under pressure at a high temperature.

Ammonia is used as a component in many industrial processes. In the Ostwald process ammonia is used to prepare nitric acid. The Solvay process uses ammonia in the production of sodium bicarbonate and sodium carbonate. Ammonia can be added directly to the soil to act as a fertilizer. A solution of ammonia is used extensively as a household cleaning agent for removing stains and grease.

Ammonia is also used to produce ammonium compounds, to manufacture nitric acid, and to dissolve certain substances.

The chemical formula for ammonia is NH_3. V. B. I.

SEE ALSO: HABER PROCESS, REFRIGERATION

Amoeba see Ameba

Amorphous carbon see Carbon

Ampere (AM-peer) The ampere is the most commonly used unit for measuring the strength of an electric current. It is the amount of current that one volt of electron-moving force can send through a resistance of one OHM. It gets its name from the French scientist ANDRE AMPERE, who lived from 1775 to 1836. The strength of the current in a television set is about one and one-half amperes. An ordinary electric BULB uses about one-half an ampere. An electric iron requires about ten amperes.

An ampere is equal to a flow of one COULOMB per second, where the coulomb is a quantity of ELECTRICITY equal to the charge on 6.25 x 10^{18} electrons. The ampere has been standardized so that it is the steady current which deposits silver at the rate of 0.001118 grams per second when passed through a silver nitrate solution.

It is helpful to distinguish between a quantity itself and its flow or rate. A container may be filled with ten gallons of water (quantity) but a faucet may deliver a gallon of water per minute (rate). Similarly, there is a coulomb of electricity (quantity) and an ampere (rate). I. K. F.

SEE ALSO: ELECTRON, MEASUREMENT, RESISTANCE, VOLT

Ampère, André Marie (1775-1836) André Ampère was a French physicist and mathematician. He was one of the most important men the world of science has ever known. In fact, he has been called the "Newton of electricity" because he identified magnetism and electricity, just as ISAAC NEWTON formulated the laws of gravity. The term "ampere," a unit of current, was named for André Ampère.

Ampère was born in Lyons, France, but he was raised in the small town of Polymieux. His father, who was almost his only teacher, cultivated in him a burning desire to understand every area of physical science. Ampère himself was interested in poetry, literature, and philosophy, but these he had to learn by himself. In 1793, Ampère's father was guillotined, and it was several years before he could overcome his grief.

In 1814, however, Ampère was elected to the Academy of Science for his outstanding work in mathematics. His area of research was problems of probability, or games of chance. Even though he gained fame as a mathematician, he continued to ponder the science of ELECTRICITY, which at that time was new and weak. He used his apartment as a laboratory, and he built his own apparatus. In spite of these hardships, Ampère made his discoveries, and he made them in a few days in a fever of activity. With André Ampère, the whole new science of electrodynamics was born.

The name "electrodynamics" comes from two Greek words, *electro,* meaning "amber," and denoting electric or electrical; and *dynamics,* meaning "powerful." Dynamics can be defined as that branch of MECHANICS concerned with the motion of bodies and the action of forces in producing or changing their motion.

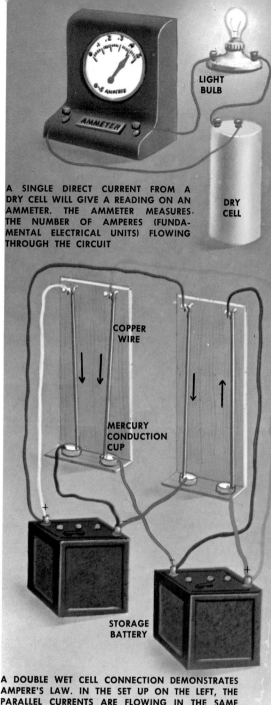

A SINGLE DIRECT CURRENT FROM A DRY CELL WILL GIVE A READING ON AN AMMETER. THE AMMETER MEASURES THE NUMBER OF AMPERES (FUNDAMENTAL ELECTRICAL UNITS) FLOWING THROUGH THE CIRCUIT

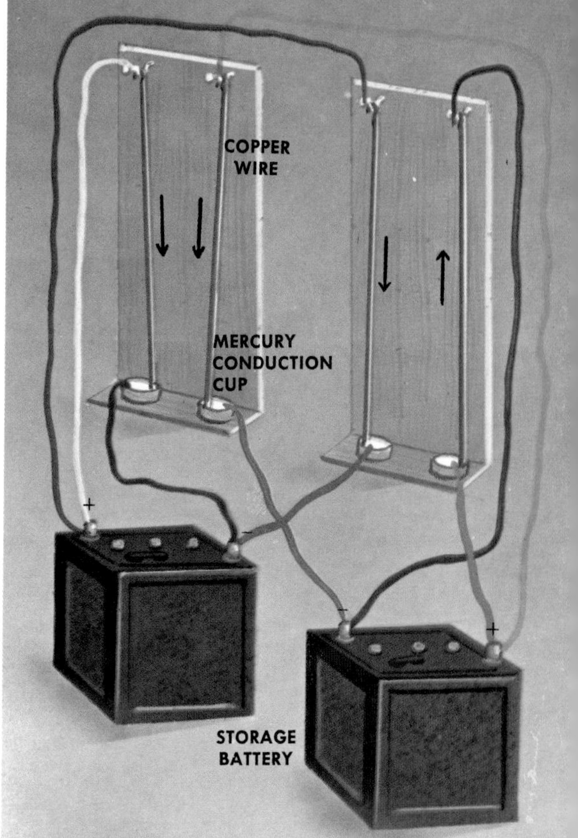

A DOUBLE WET CELL CONNECTION DEMONSTRATES AMPERE'S LAW. IN THE SET UP ON THE LEFT, THE PARALLEL CURRENTS ARE FLOWING IN THE SAME DIRECTION. THE COPPER WIRES ARE ATTRACTED TO EACH OTHER. ON THE RIGHT, THE CURRENT FLOW IS OPPOSITE AND THE COPPER WIRES ARE REPELLED

Ampere's law states: two parallel currents having the same direction attract each other, and two parallel currents having opposite directions repel each other. He proved that electrical currents have the same effects as MAGNETS. As a result, he invented the astatic needle, which has made it possible to detect and measure electric current. An astatic needle is one that is not fixed in one position or one direction. D. H. J.

Amphibians Amphibians are animals that live a "double life." Their eggs are laid in water, and they spend the first part of their lives in water. The young amphibians are called LARVAE or tadpoles. When they are tadpoles, amphibians live like fish. When they grow up they are able to live on land. When they are adults they are more like reptiles. FROGS, TOADS, NEWTS, and SALAMANDERS are amphibians.

Amphibia are divided into four smaller groups (orders), but only two of these are common in North America. Frogs and toads are tailless. Adults live on land, returning to the water to reproduce. Males fertilize eggs as they are laid by the female. Fertilized eggs (zygotes) develop in the water into tailed, gilled tadpoles.

In the second group are the tailed salamanders and newts. Some salamanders never lose their gills, other develop lungs, while some breathe only through their skins. Many spend their entire lives in water. Some of those with lungs live for several years on land and then return to water. In the land stage they are called efts.

Amphibians are back-boned animals, or *vertebrates*. Some of them have soft, moist skin and some have soft, dry skin. They are called "cold-blooded" animals because the temperature of their bodies depends on the temperature of their surroundings. When they are in a cold place, their bodies are cold, but when they are in a warm place, their bodies are warm. Tadpoles and some salamanders have the power of REGENERATION, which means that if they lose a part of their bodies, such as a tail, they are able to grow a new one.

The eggs of the amphibian are deposited in water and are surrounded by a jelly-like substance for protection. The eggs develop into a larval or tadpole stage. During this period they live in water and breathe through gills, just as fish do. At this stage they do

not have legs but they propel themselves by their tails. As amphibians enter the next period of their lives they grow legs. In some cases, such as with frogs and most toads, the tails become shorter and eventually disappear. Their gills are replaced by lungs, and they are then ready to move out of the water and live on land.

The life history of these creatures represents the history of the slow EVOLUTION of all land vertebrates, beginning in water and graduating to land-living. Most amphibians must return to the water, however, in order to begin again their reproductive cycle.

Amphibians without tails are either *frogs* or *toads*. Sometimes it is difficult to tell a frog from a toad. Usually frogs have smooth, moist skin and are rather slender. Toads have rough, warty, dry skin and are squatty. The bodies of frogs and toads are short. Their front legs are short, but their back legs are long. Their long back legs help them to be good jumpers. The tongues of most animals are fastened to the backs of their mouths. Frogs and toads, however, have their tongues attached to the front of their mouths. Their tongues are very sticky. If an insect comes near a frog in the morning, the frog throws out his long, sticky tongue and catches the insect for his breakfast. Perhaps the frog would call it supper, though, for frogs and toads are more active during the night. They rest during the day. Frogs and toads usually hibernate in the winter.

Newts and *salamanders* are the amphibians with tails. Some of them have only two legs. Some species of newts and salamanders keep their gills as well as their tails from the tadpole stage. Newts are usually smaller than salamanders and their skin is a little rougher and not as slippery as the salamander's skin. Salamanders are sometimes rather slimy.

Some people believe that amphibians are poisonous and that handling toads will give a person warts. These ideas are false.

Amphibians are very useful creatures. Although the larvae are vegetarians, adult amphibians eat insects. They eliminate many insects that would destroy crops. They also help to keep down the number of annoying and germ-carrying insects such as flies and mosquitoes. Some of the frog species provide a food delicacy for man—frogs' legs. Amphibians are also used extensively in the laboratory for scientific experiments and research. C. L. K.

SEE ALSO: METAMORPHOSIS

Amphioxus see Chordata

Amphoterism see Acids and bases

Amplifier see Radio

Amplitude see Sound

Amundsen, Roald (1872-1928) Amundsen was a famous Norwegian explorer. He was the first man to visit both the North and South Poles. He had hoped to be first to the North Pole, but American ROBERT E. PEARY reached it first. Amundsen and his men raced Englishman R. F. Scott to the South Pole and Amundsen's expedition won. Amundsen raised the flag of Norway at the South Pole on December 14, 1911.

Amundsen was born near Oslo, Norway. He studied medicine for a while but then changed to the study of navigation. He first sailed with a Norwegian Navy ship headed for the Antarctic. Later, as captain, he led the first ship through the Northwest Passage across North America from the Atlantic to the Pacific.

In 1910, Amundsen let his crew believe they were heading for the North Pole, even though Peary had already reached it. At sea, he announced to his men that they were going to the South Pole and that Scott and his English crew were already heading there. The men cheered and the race was on.

When they reached the Bay of Wales, Amundsen and his men set up camp to wait for spring before continuing to the South Pole. During the winter, they ventured out to set up supply houses at intervals along the route to the Pole. When weather finally permitted, Amundsen and four men set out by lightly-loaded dogsled, skimming from one supply station to the next, and reached the South Pole. They left a note for the Scott expedition with their flag.

Although Amundsen was not the first to reach the North Pole, he thought he could obtain valuable scientific information by flying over the Pole. After an attempt in a single-engine plane that smashed its landing gear, he successfully crossed the North Pole in dirigible *Norge,* in 1926. He raced the Italian explorer Umberto Nobile and there was some dispute over who was first.

After Amundsen retired, Nobile became lost on another trip to the Arctic in 1928. Amundsen set out to look for him. Nobile was found by another search party, but Amundsen was lost and never returned from that last expedition to the polar regions. C. L. K.

Amylase (AM-eh-laz) Amylase is a material or chemical made by living cells. It is used to break down food into small molecules that can be used by the body. The amylase in saliva changes starch into sugar.

In humans the salivary glands and pancreas produce amylases to aid in the digestion of carbohydrates. These enzymes produce chemical reactions by adding water to glycogen causing it to split up into glucose. Starch digestion begins in the mouth and is finished by the pancreatic amylase in the small intestine. H. J. C.

SEE ALSO: DIGESTIVE SYSTEM

Anaconda see Snakes

Anaesthetic see Anesthetic

Analog computer see Computer

Analytic geometry see Geometry

©Parke-Davis & Company

Anatomy Anatomy is the structure or form of any body. Anatomy is often used to mean the structure of the human body. However, all plants and animals have form, so that plant anatomy and animal anatomy are also studied as sciences.

When men first began to think about how living bodies are formed, their only tool was the dissecting knife. ARISTOTLE, in ancient Greece, observed and described chick eggs developing. Galen, a physician in Alexandria in Roman times, did careful dissections of apes and lower animals in order to understand the human body. But it was very dangerous to do dissections because people of ancient times were frightened about destroying the soul, and there were laws forbidding it.

During the 15th and 16th centuries, the invention of the printed book, the great revival of interest in art, and a new feeling of the importance of man made anatomy a topic of investigation once again. The artist LEONARDO DA VINCI made a detailed study of anatomical structures. Andreas Vesalius published a great classic work that made him known as "the father of modern anatomy."

BRANCHES OF ANATOMY

There was another great advance in anatomy when the MICROSCOPE was invented. It was then possible to study not only gross anatomy, the structures seen with the naked eye, but also the anatomy of very small structures that could be seen now under the microscope. *Histology,* the study of tissues, and *cytology,* the study of cells, came into being. With the invention of the electron microscope one can see details in very small cellular structures. The anatomy of such small bodies as bacteria, viruses, genes and the mitochondria of the cell can now be understood.

Because every form has a function or use in the body, a true knowledge of anatomy requires an understanding of *physiology.* In order to understand the mature form and how it came into existence, scientists began the study of development, or *embryology.* The descriptive anatomy of each form suggested that various forms of plants and animals should be compared. Comparative anatomy has had a tremendous significance in providing evidence for the theory of evolution. The discovery of homologous structures, those that have a common origin, and analogous structures, those that are similar only in appearance or use, has given a basis for classifying plants and animals into related groups, the science of TAXONOMY.

So that further information could be learned about the structure of the body, scientists performed experiments to change the existing anatomical relationships and discover what would happen. This very advanced stage of study is called *experimental anatomy.*

A new outlook became necessary in order to bring together all the knowledge from each of these fields. The name *morphology,* or science of form, is now given to this branch of learning.

THE SYSTEMS OF THE HUMAN BODY

The head, the chest, the back, the trunk, the arm, and the leg all name parts of the body that are easily recognized. But the size, place and relationships of the parts inside as well as outside the body are so important that anatomy is usually studied as a group of systems, or related structures.

The body can be thought of as a neat package containing many parts. These special parts are tied and packed together in such a way that they work well without taking up any extra room. The *cells* that perform the same kind of work are wrapped together as *tissues.* Tissues that work together are wrapped as *organs.* They are wrapped in membranes that support and protect them as they grow and function. *Systems* are formed of organs working together. B. B. G.

SEE ALSO: AUTONOMIC NERVOUS SYSTEM, CELL, CIRCULATORY SYSTEM, DIGESTIVE SYSTEM, ENDOCRINE GLANDS, EXCRETORY SYSTEM, HISTOLOGY, LYMPHATIC SYSTEM, MUSCLE SYSTEM, NERVOUS SYSTEM, PHYSIOLOGY, REPRODUCTIVE SYSTEM, RESPIRATORY SYSTEM, SKELETON, SKIN

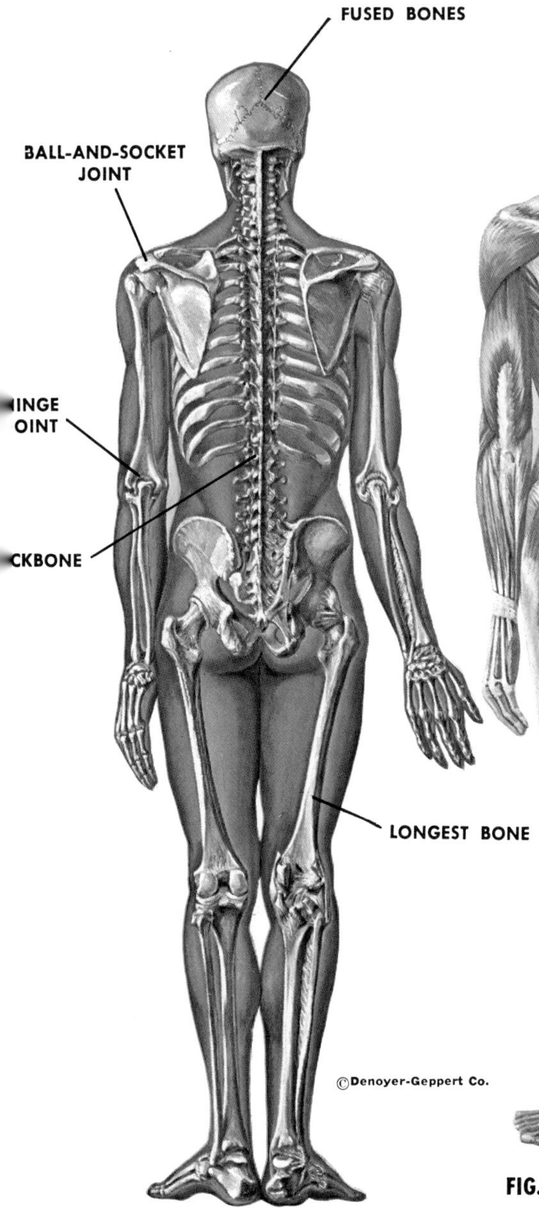

FIG. 1. SKELETON

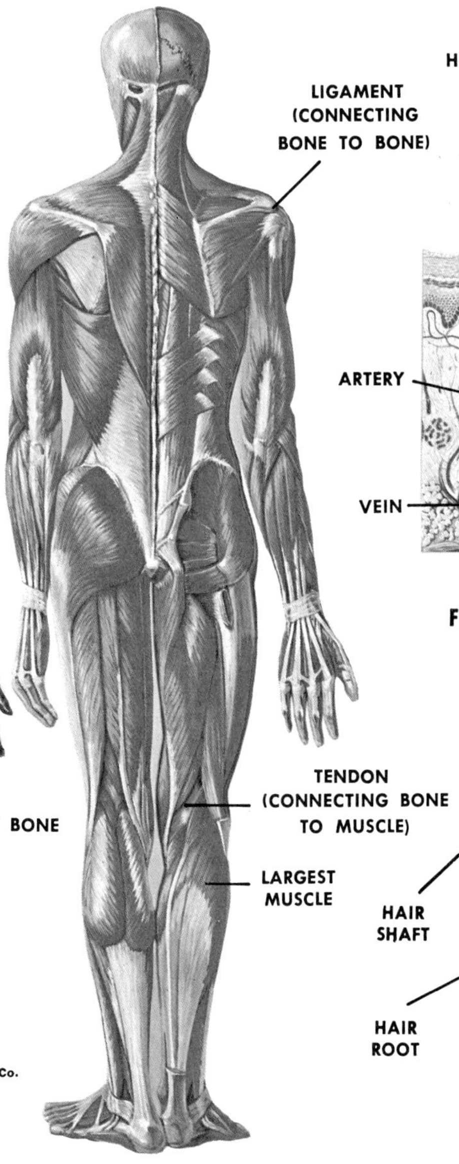

FIG. 2. MUSCULATURE

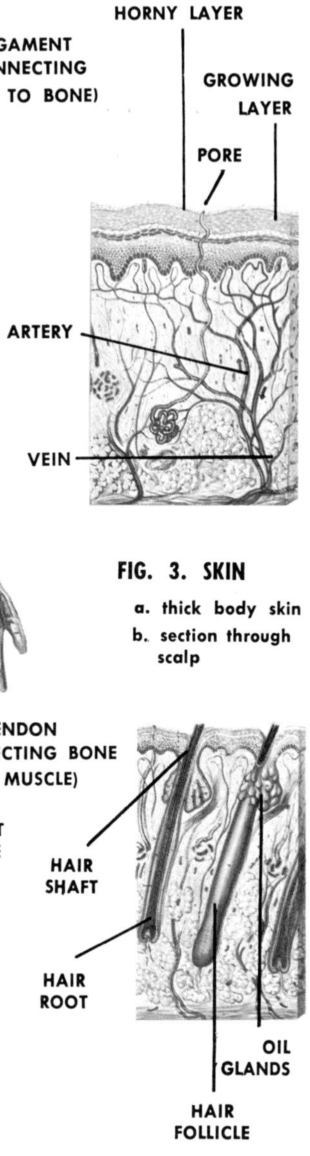

FIG. 3. SKIN

a. thick body skin

b. section through scalp

Fig. 1. The skeleton is the support of the body. It is made up of many large and small bones. The moving joints connecting the bones make possible both large and delicate motions of the body

Fig. 2. The muscles control the movements of the body. They are made of fibers which contract and pull. Muscles are anchored to the bones by tendons.

Fig. 3. The skin is a strong elastic sheet that covers the body. It contains special organs that protect delicate internal structures. Oil and sweat glands close to the surface release substances that keep the skin healthy. Skin grows from the inside as the outer layers wear off

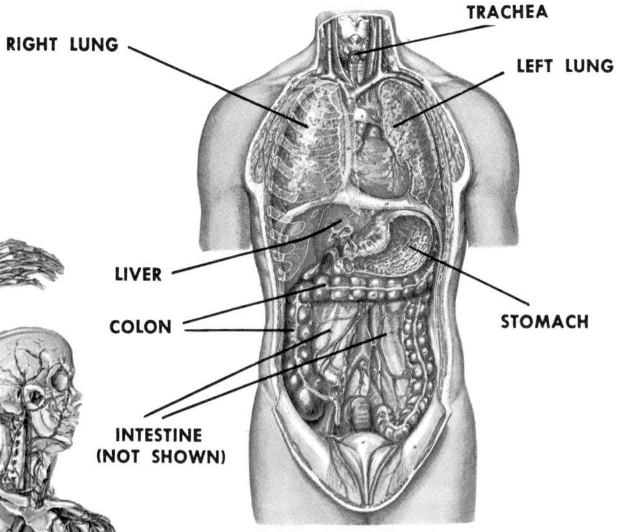

FIG. 5. DIGESTIVE AND RESPIRATORY SYSTEMS

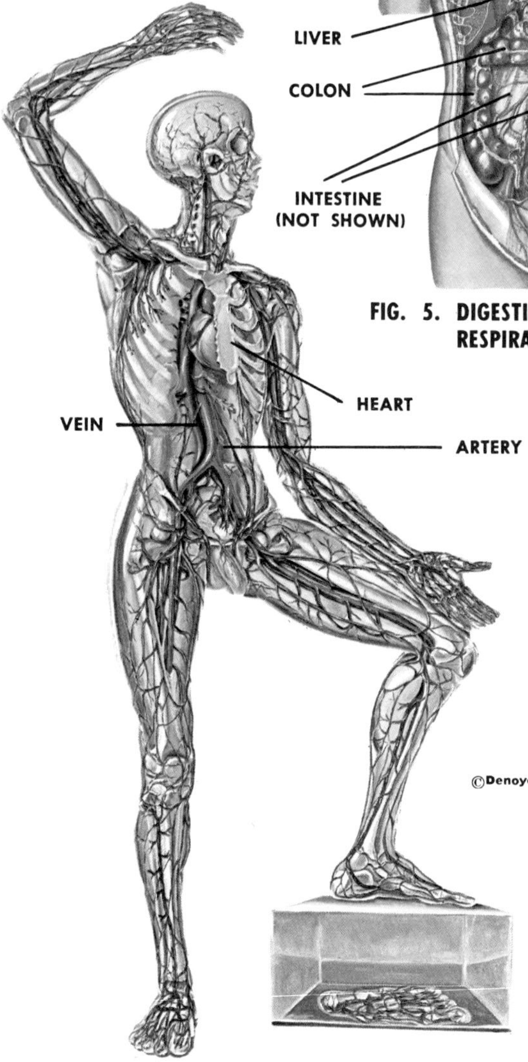

FIG. 4. CIRCULATORY SYSTEM

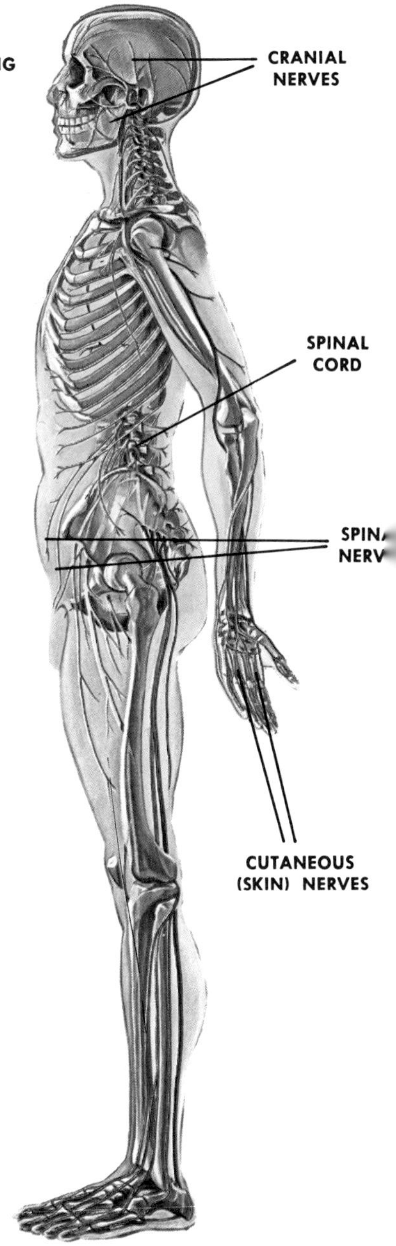

FIG. 6. NERVOUS SYSTEM

Fig. 4. The circulatory system is a complex network of blood vessels. Most arteries carry the blood, containing food and oxygen, from the heart to the body. Most veins return it to the heart

Fig. 5. The organs of the digestive system collect, prepare and digest the food so that the body can use it. The respiratory system includes the organs that work to supply the body with oxygen. It goes from nose to the tiny alveoli of the lungs where an exchange of O_2 and CO_2 occurs

Fig. 6. Messages that coordinate the many different parts of the body travel along the branching nervous system. Sense organs supply information about the inside and the outside of the body. The spinal cord and brain collect, interpret and answer

Anchovy (ANN-tchoh-vee) Anchovy is the name of many small SARDINE-like fishes related to the HERRING. The most common are found off the coast of southern Europe. When dried and salted, they have a strong, special flavor.

Andes Mountains see South America

Androgen Androgens are hormones that affect the body tissues so that male characteristics appear. *Testosterone* has been studied the most; it is produced by the male gonads (testes). Adrenal glands of both sexes make other androgens. Chemically, androgens are all steroids.
SEE: GONAD, REPRODUCTIVE SYSTEMS, TESTIS

Anemia Anemia is a physical condition caused by a lack of *hemoglobin* in the blood. Hemoglobin is a red protein which carries oxygen to all body cells. In anemia, the red cells which carry hemoglobin either are too few in number or do not contain enough hemoglobin.

Because there is not enough red BLOOD pigment and/or cells, the anemic person is often pale. Other signs of anemia are shortness of breath and a feeling of weakness. Mental work is tiring for an anemic person because not enough oxygen reaches the brain. Anemia also lowers the body's resistance to other diseases.

There are three main types of anemia: 1) anemia caused by the loss of blood, 2) anemia caused by destruction of the red blood cells, 3) anemia caused by defective blood formation.

A severe hemorrhage or chronic bleeding, as from an ulcer, results in anemia due to blood loss.

Anemia due to the destruction of red blood cells may be inherited, as in the case of sickle-cell anemia. Destruction of the red corpuscles may also be caused by poisons, infectious bacteria, or blood parasites. Snake venom, scarlet fever, and malaria produce this type of anemia.

Anemia caused by defective blood formation may be a nutritional or a metabolic disorder. A diet lacking in iron, an element necessary for the production of hemoglobin, causes anemia. Even when iron is present in the diet, anemia will result if the metabolism is faulty so that the body is unable to utilize iron in the formation of the hemoglobin molecule.

When cancerous growths or scar tissue take up space in the bone marrow, where red blood cells are produced, fewer red cells can be formed, and anemia results. Radiation from X-rays or radioactive materials can also destroy the cells of the marrow, so that red blood cells can no longer be made.

Some types of anemia can be corrected or improved by adding liver, iron, or vitamin B_{12} to the diet. Sometimes blood transfusions are necessary. Serious anemia may result in death. I. H. S.

Anemometer (an-uh-MOM-muh-ter) The anemometer is an instrument which tells how fast the wind is blowing. Airplane pilots and sailors need to know the speed of the wind. They must also know the direction of the wind.

Some anemometers can show the direction and speed of the wind at the same time. These look like small airplanes placed on top of a pole. Other kinds of anemometers look like whirling cups on top of a high post. The anemometers must be high above the ground and away from anything that might stop the flow of air. The weather man needs to use an anemometer as he makes his weather forecasts.

There are several kinds of anemometers in use today. Each type is used for a special need. The rotating one (whirling cups) is a *Robinson* anemometer. It is commonly used at airports and weather stations. This type is frequently used because it works well under

✳ **THINGS TO DO**

WHAT IS THE SPEED OF MOVING AIR AT ANY GIVEN TIME OF DAY?

Materials: two hollow rubber balls cut in half, dowel rods, wooden support

1 **Assemble the materials according to the illustration. Nail the halves of the balls on the ends of the two sticks.**
2 **Drill a hole in the top of the wooden support a little larger than the nail used in cross arms. Wax the inside of the hole to cut down on friction. Candle drippings may be used.**
3 **Paint one cup a different color to make counting easier.**
4 **To determine the wind velocity (miles per hour), count the number of revolutions in thirty seconds and divide by five.**

a great number of conditions. The Robinson device is unlike the windmill or propeller types because it measures wind velocities without having to turn directly into the wind. The wind speed is determined by the rotation of the cup wheel on the time base. The speed of the wind is measured by the number of turns of the wheel in a certain length of time.

The *hot wire* anemometer is used when it is necessary to obtain very accurate readings of wind speed. The *pressure plate* anemometer is another type which is often used in industry and in weather studies which require exact recording of air speeds. D. E. Z.

SEE ALSO: WEATHER FORECASTING, WIND

Anemone see Wild flowers

Aneroid barometer see Barometer

Anesthetics (ann-uhs-THET-ticks) Anesthetics are chemical substances that affect nerves. They cause a loss of feeling with or without loss of consciousness (thinking power). A skinned knee, a cut finger, and a headache make a person feel pain. To lessen pain people take pain-relievers, like aspirin, or rub the affected area with liniment. Some mild pain relievers lessen pain. Stronger anesthetics are used before and during SURGERY.

Besides lessening pain, anesthetics serve other purposes. They reduce or eliminate REFLEX activity and relax muscles. They may be used to induce unconsciousness. Therefore, surgical operations can be performed effectively.

There are two kinds of anesthetics, *general* and *local. General* anesthetics are used when complete loss of consciousness is desired. They are most often used in operations on deep-lying organs or the abdomen.

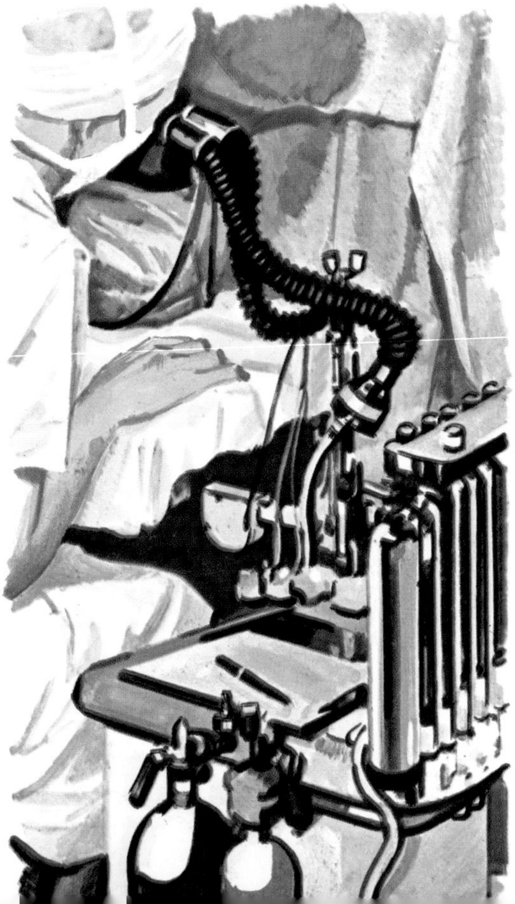

Some general anesthetics are given by having the patient inhale through a mask such *volatile* chemicals as ETHER, nitrous oxide, halothane, fluothane, and cyclopropamide. The original successful anesthetic, CHLOROFORM, is no longer used because it can damage the liver. *Nonvolatile* general anesthetics, such as sodium pentothal or paraldehyde, are given by vein or rectum. All general anesthetics work by traveling through the bloodstream to the brain, where they suppress conscious thinking, or "put the patient to sleep."

Local anesthetics are used when only a particular region of the body is to be affected. They do not cause unconsciousness. Many people mistakenly assume that local anesthetics can be used only in minor surgery. But certain local anesthetics are effective in abdominal surgery, amputations, and childbirth. Spinal and nerve blocks are produced by local anesthetics. Dentists use local anesthetics, especially novocain, when extracting and filling teeth. Many advances in surgery have resulted from a growing knowledge of anesthetics.

E. S. S. /G. A. D.

Angiosperms (AN-gee-oh-sperm) Two Greek words were put together to form the name for a large group of plants with flowers. The word *angeion* means "cover" and the word *sperma* means "seed." Together these words make the name "angiosperm," which describes all the plants that have seeds inside a covering. The seeds in a peach blossom are inside a covering called an ovary. When most flower parts die the ovary grows and becomes the fruit which is called a peach. All angiosperms have roots, stems, leaves, flowers, seeds and fruits. Most of the plants in the world belong to this group. For example, a maple tree, a rose bush, a wild violet, and a stalk of wheat are all angiosperms.

Angiosperms are usually *terrestrial,* which means they live on land. Lower plants still need water for reproduction in order to bring about the union of the egg and sperm. In higher plants the POLLEN is carried to the

WILD LILY

CORN

BANANA

YUCCA

FORSYTHIA

Courtesy Society For Visual Education, Inc.

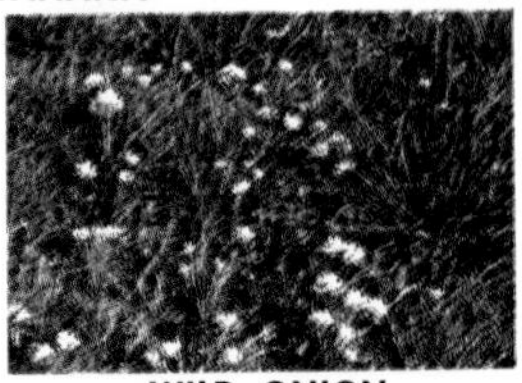

WILD ONION

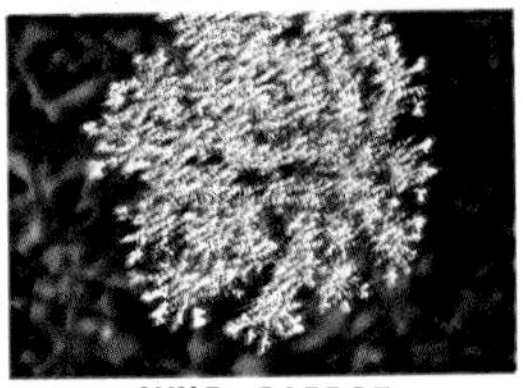

WILD CARROT

All angiosperms have roots, leaves, flowers, seeds, and fruits

egg by the wind or by an animal. Therefore, angiosperms live in a wide variety of places, on high mountains, on deserts, and in the hot tropical regions. They are generally upright plants. They are independent because they contain CHLOROPHYLL which is necessary for a plant to make its own food. They have special tubes (VASCULAR BUNDLES) inside the plant parts which carry the raw materials up to the leaves and the food back down to all parts. This is another advantage that has allowed the angiosperms to advance beyond the lowly green plants of the world called ALGAE.

Angiosperms are divided into two groups according to characteristics in their structure. The first group, called MONOCOTYLEDONS (one seed-leaf), makes up twenty-five per cent of the flowering plants. The veins in their leaves are parallel or linear, and the flower parts are in multiples of three. One may observe a tulip specimen in order to understand the structure of a "monocot." The veins in the long slender leaves extend from the top to the bottom. The tulip has six petals and six stamens. The seeds are enclosed in a single ovary. Since the seed cannot be separated into two halves it has one cotyledon. Examples of monocots are grasses, palms, iris, narcissus, trillium, orchids and many others of similar structure.

The second group of angiosperms is called DICOTYLEDONS, meaning "having two seed leaves." Dicots include seventy-five per cent of the most familiar flowering plants. The broad leaves have veins which form a network within the whole blade. This type of venation is further classified into *pinnate* and *palmate*. The flower parts are usually in multiples of two or five. The violet plant with its five petals and five stamens is an example. The leaf is broad with the veins branching out in all directions from the petiole. When the flower dies and the seed is mature within the ripened ovary or fruit, it is possible to separate the little seeds into two halves or cotyledons. Most of the broad-leafed trees, annuals, and other perennials are in subclass *Dicotyledoneae*. H. J. C.

SEE ALSO: LEAVES, TRACHEOPHYTE

Angles see Geometry

Angleworm see Earthworm

Angstrom see Light, Measurement, Wave

Anhydride (an-HY-dride) Oxides which unite with water to form bases or acids are known as anhydrides. Nearly all non-metals and several metal elements form anhydrides. The elements whose oxides form acids when combined with water are classed as *non-metals*. The elements whose oxides form bases when placed in water are classed as METALS.

The acid radicals which remain after the water has been abstracted from the acid are known as acid anhydrides. Oxides which unite with water to form bases are known as basic anhydrides.

A few elements are on the borderline between metals and non-metals. The oxides of copper do not react with water and so form neither an acid or a base when placed with water. W. J. K.

SEE ALSO: ACIDS AND BASES, ELEMENTS, OXIDE

Animal You can easily hold more than a thousand animals in one hand. You can do this by holding a spoon of water from a pond. In the water are many tiny animals too small to see without a microscope. The largest animal on earth is the blue whale which can grow to a length of over 100 feet (30.48 meters) and may weigh over 100 tons (90.72 metric tons). The ELEPHANT is the largest land animal. The OSTRICH is the largest bird.

The tiniest and the largest animals are alike in several ways. All animals need *oxygen*. Some get it from the air, some from water, and others from the soil. Plants manufacture their own food, but all animals depend upon plants or other animals for their food. All animals have ways to *digest* food and remove waste materials. All animals can *move*. Even animals which attach themselves to the ocean bottom or rocks can move a little in getting food or protecting themselves.

The polar bear and the penguin like to live in cold regions. Lions and tigers make their homes in warm jungles and bush country. The elk and the squirrel live where there are both cold and warm seasons. The gila monster and the horned toad are suited to life in dry regions. The monkey and the leopard are found in forests while the zebra and the rhinoceros live on the plains.

Animals that do not seem to be at all alike often live in the same areas. There are so many animals living in different places, and there is so much to know about them, the story of animals is long.

Cardinals do not migrate in winter.

n R. Nickles; National Fish & Wildlife Service

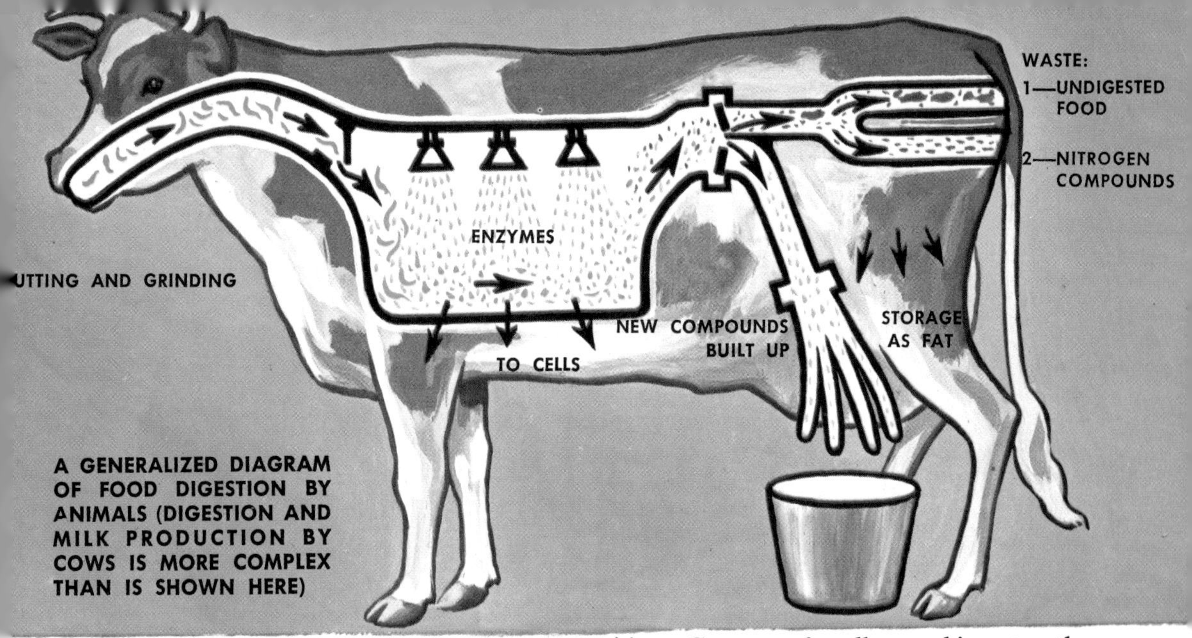

HOW ANIMALS ARE BUILT

Any one kind of animal looks different from most other animals. The housefly looks somewhat like a bird, but not at all like a porcupine or kangaroo. They are alike because they are built of the same material.

All animals, like all plants, are built mainly of a material called *protoplasm*. Protoplasm is arranged into cells, divided from one another by means of a partition, much as the rooms of a house are divided by walls. Food must be supplied to protoplasm in order to replace the worn-out cells and manufacture new ones. Just as in a house, repairs must be made and new rooms built to take care of new members of the family.

A few animals consist of only one tiny cell. The AMEBA and the PARAMECIUM are microscopic examples of one-celled animals. They belong to a group of animals called PROTOZOA. Many scientists believe that simple one-celled animals were the first to appear on the earth.

Every cell, whether a whole animal or part of one, has a tough, jelly-like outer covering which is porous like a screen. Food and waste can pass back and forth through the pores of this elastic membrane.

Most animals are built of many cells. When the animal is made of many cells, the cells must work together in teams to more efficiently take care of the many body activities. Groups of cells working together, doing the same work are called *tissues*. Group of tissues working together to perform special jobs are called *organs*. The heart and the brain are organs made up of groups of tissues. Organs work together to form *systems* which run throughout the body to circulate food, gases, and waste products. Large animals have complicated systems, such as the NERVOUS SYSTEM which carries messages and the RESPIRATORY SYSTEM which exchanges oxygen and carbon dioxide.

HOW ANIMALS GET THEIR FOOD

Unlike plants, animals are not able to manufacture the food necessary to keep them alive. Therefore, animals must eat plants or other animals that have eaten plants.

Animals get their food in many different and strange ways. The ameba wraps itself around its food and takes it into its body in a large sac called a *food vacuole*. The EARTHWORM swallows soil as it burrows its way underground and then digests the plant and animal life in the soil before passing it out of its body. The female MOSQUITO lives on a diet of blood which it sucks through the skin of mammals. The clothes MOTH and CRICKET eat clothing as well. Both are really after the organic substances in soiled clothing.

North American forest dwellers.

North American desert animals.

North American Arctic animals.

Warm-water sea dwellers.

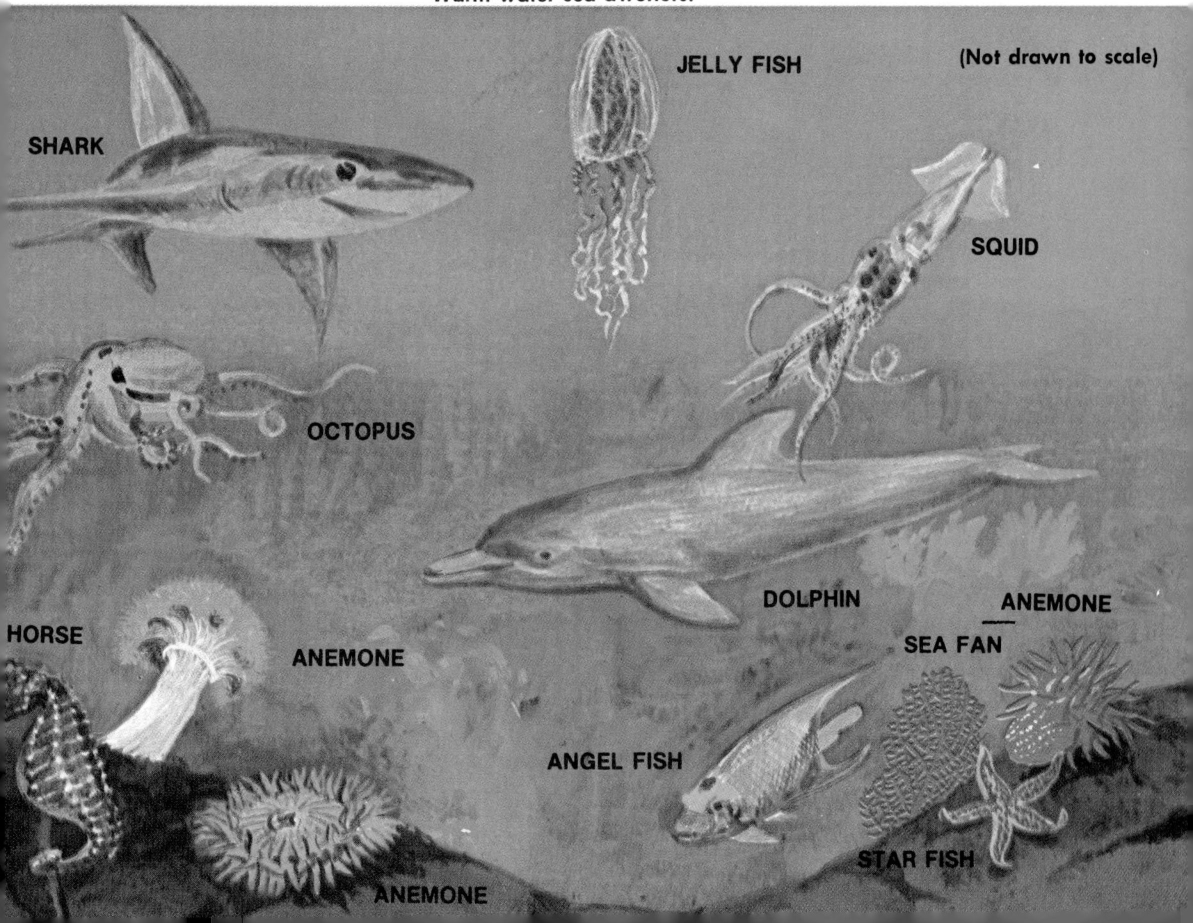

The BEE makes its food from the perfumed nectar of flowers It takes the nectar into its body. There it collects it, pre-digests it, and vomits it into the receptacles of the honeycomb at the hive to be stored for winter.

Some SNAKES swallow small animals whole. Some poison their prey first. Toads, frogs, and salamanders eat insects, catching them with a quick flick of their long tongues. Most birds eat plant seeds and insects. The young birds usually are fed a diet of insects and later learn to eat grass and weed seeds. The beaks of birds are shaped to gather these two kinds of food.

The camel, horse, buffalo and deer are vegetarians. They eat grass, leaves, and other soft parts of plants. The lion, tiger and wolf eat other animals. All have bodies that can spring quickly on prey after a stealthy approach. Most whales eat tiny plants and animals called ALGAE and PLANKTON which they strain out of the great amounts of sea water which pass through their bodies. Is it not strange that the largest of animals eats some of the smallest plants and animals?

HOW ANIMALS DIGEST THEIR FOOD

No matter how an animal gets its food, all animals must be equipped for using the food once it is in the body. Every animal must also have certain kinds of food. They must have CARBOHYDRATES, FATS and PROTEINS. These are gotten by eating plants and other animals. The foods are broken down (digested) into simpler substances. These are used by cells to release the ENERGY necessary for life activities such as movement or secretion.

The large pieces of raw food must be broken down into tiny molecules which can pass through the membrane of the cell and be used by the protoplasm. Carbohydrates are broken into STARCHES and SUGARS, fats into FATTY ACIDS, and proteins into AMINO ACIDS. To assist in the breakdown of the food, ENZYMES are present in the body. These are *catalysts,* which hurry the breakdown but do not change themselves. This process is called *digestion.*

The food must be burned so that energy may be released. The burning of any material requires oxygen. This process takes place in the cells of the body. The oxygen is obtained from the atmosphere or water. In animals like the protozoans or sponges, which have one or only a few cells, the cells are in contact with the environment and oxygen may be taken in directly. In more complex animals, there must be a special structure to circulate the oxygen throughout the body.

The building blocks of proteins, amino acids, when broken down produce the waste material ammonia. This material, produced within the protoplasm of the cell, is poisonous and must be removed at once or changed to a less poisonous form like urea. This is passed out through a special organ called a nephridium or KIDNEY. The process is excretion.

HOW ANIMALS MOVE

Most animals can move from one place to another. They need to move to find both food and mates, to protect themselves against their enemies, and to protect themselves when the weather is too hot or too cold.

Some ways of moving may be seen among animals which have one cell. Most of these animals live in water. They have special devices for moving. Some larger animals move in the same way. The ameba moves by extending the protoplasm of its cell into a long foot-like projection. This is called a *pseudopod.* The contents of the cell flow gradually into the pseudopod and the animal moves forward.

The EUGLENA has a single thread or whip, called a *flagellum,* which is attached to one end of the animal. This is lashed through the water and the animal is towed behind it. Some animals have beating *cilia,* which are hair-like threads of protoplasm, extending from the cell or cells.

Many animals move by means of *muscles,* which allow them to creep or walk on land, to swim in the water or to fly in the air. Creeping animals, like the CLAM, are slow in movement. They have claws, bristles or suckers which, when pushed along a fairly solid surface, create friction and allow the animal to hold to the surface.

Small animals serve as food for larger animals. Both the large and small have devices, such as claws and special coloring, to protect them from their enemies

Many land animals have jointed legs which support the body and lift it off the ground. These animals are able to move very fast. Some aquatic animals, like fish, have wide, flat appendages which, when moved back and forth, act like paddles to propel the animal. Other aquatic animals, like the OCTOPUS, move by "jet propulsion." Water is taken in, then forced out through an opening with great force. Bats, most birds and insects have wings which propel them through the air. Movement from one place to another is called *locomotion*.

HOW ANIMALS PROTECT THEMSELVES

The way in which an animal protects itself depends upon the type of body it has, its home, its enemies and many other factors. Many specific ways by which animals protect themselves can be seen throughout the animal kingdom.

Animals can: (1) move quickly—BIRD, RABBIT: (2) hide by camouflage or PROTECTIVE COLORING—CHAMELEON; (3) attack the enemy with special devices—TIGER, BEE; (4) spray bad-smelling or opaque chemicals—SKUNK, SQUID; (5) leave spiny objects in the skin of the attacking animal—PORCUPINE; (6) migrate or hibernate to escape winter weather—goose, FROG; or (7) build homes against enemies—SQUIRREL, man.

The basic thing an animal can do for protection, however, is to *respond* to the things around it. The things it can feel, smell, hear, see and taste tell it when it is in danger. Each animal is able to respond in some way to warnings from its surroundings, or environment, and from inside itself. The way in which it responds is different for different animals.

HOW ANIMALS REPRODUCE

When a person wears a hole through the bottom of his shoes, he can buy a new pair. There are factories which make shoes, so that new ones will be ready when the old ones wear out. Animals are like shoe factories. They can always make more animals just like themselves. Animal bodies wear out or are killed. New ones must always be ready.

Animals are able to produce new individuals. This is important, not for the life of the particular animal, but for the continued life of the group of animals. Some of the one-celled animals, like the ameba, are able to produce a new individual by dividing into two parts. Other animals, like the sponge, produce large lumps or buds on the body that separate and develop into new individuals. In some animals groups, there are two sexes present. The individual animals are members of either the male or the female sex or both—HERMAPHRODITE. In each sex, there are cells specialized for producing new animals. When the male and female mate, they each contribute one or more sex cells which fuse and a new animal begins to develop. Sometimes, the cell grows inside the female animal, just as puppies grow inside the body of the mother dog. Sometimes, the animal develops outside of the female, as does the chicken, which is hatched from an egg. Production of new animals is called *reproduction*. E.P.L.

SEE ALSO: ANATOMY; ANIMALS, CLASSIFICATION OF; CIRCULATORY SYSTEM; DIGESTIVE SYSTEM; EVOLUTION; PHYSIOLOGY; REPRODUCTION, ASEXUAL; REPRODUCTIVE SYSTEM; RESPIRATORY SYSTEM

✳ THINGS TO DO

MAKING CAGES FOR SMALL MAMMALS

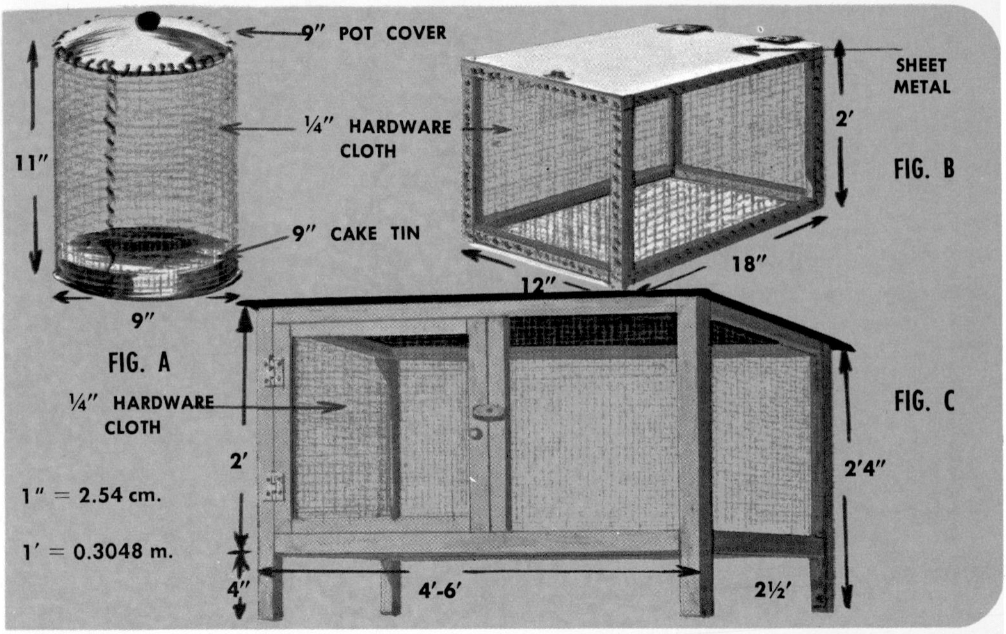

A Materials: 11-inch by 30-inch hardware cloth of ¼-inch mesh, 9-inch pot cover, 9-inch cake pan, 18-gauge copper wire.

1 Roll hardware cloth into a cylinder 9 inches in diameter and 11 inches high. Lace the sides with copper wire.

2 Drill holes at 3 inch intervals around the pot cover and lace it to the top of the cylinder.

3 Set the cylinder over the up-side-down cake tin. Cage is ready for use.

B Materials: Wooden framework of 1-inch square posts, ¼-inch mesh hardware cloth, wood staples, 2 pieces of sheet metal, hinges.

1 Construct cage according to illustration.

2 Use one piece of sheet metal as the floor which can be pulled out for cleaning.

C Materials: 17-gauge hardware cloth of ½-inch mesh, or ⅝-inch mesh, depending on breed; scrap lumber frame, hinges, wooden peg for lock, sheet metal or tar paper-covered wood for roof.

1 Construct according to illustration.

2 Wooden peg lock should be tight so it cannot slip.

3 If the doe is breeding, a box of straw should be put in cage for nesting.

Animal behavior An animal behaves or acts toward certain things around it. It may move or make some sign in response to other living organisms or to a physical condition.

Behaviors can be grouped into types depending upon external actions and the internal physiology of the animal. *Reflex* is a behavior that is done automatically. *Instinct* is an unlearned action by an animal. *Habituation* and *imprinting* are learned responses. Chemicals that are made by one animal and cause another animal to react are called *pheromones.*

The behavior of animals is displayed when a queen bee organizes a hive, a male fish goes through a mating ceremony to get a female to lay her eggs, or a bird fights off others to save its territory or nesting place.

More complex animal behaviors include migration, hibernation, nest building, and the sucking reflex of baby mammals. The study of behavior is popular today. A scientist in this area is an *ethologist.* H. J. C.

SEE ALSO: BABY ANIMALS

Animal cages An animal cage should be large enough to give the animal space for exercise. It should also be built so as to be easy to clean. Both space and cleanliness are important for a caged animal to stay healthy.

Different types of animals require different types of cages. Small animals, such as hamsters or gerbils, can be kept successfully in old bird or squirrel cages. A cage with an exercise wheel is useful. The female before having her young must be removed to a small individual cage. Wood shavings make good bedding material.

Since mice gnaw, they need small metal cages about 6 inches (15.24 centimeters). Large glass jars with wire mesh covers may also be used. A small wire basket to hold food can be welded to the mesh lid.

Rats need a larger cage about 18 x 12 x 4 inches (45.7 x 30.5 x 10.2 centimeters). The bottom should be mesh with a tray of shavings underneath.

The size of bird cages depends on the size of the bird. Round ones are not roomy and should not be used. J. C. K.

SEE ALSO: MAMMALIA

Animal diseases Of the more than 200 diseases of domestic animals, about 180 are similar to human diseases. Most germ diseases and accidents that affect animals have treatments either the same or very similar to those used for curing people.

Diseases such as rabies, tuberculosis, and skin tumors have long been known in animals. Ancient farmers learned about setting broken human bones from practice in splinting injured bones of their pets and livestock.

The great advances in animal medicine came only with the modern sciences, as led by such men as WILLIAM HARVEY, Claude Bernard, CHARLES DARWIN and LOUIS PASTEUR. They and many others found the similarities of all living things.

Kinds of diseases: Animal infectious diseases are grouped by causes (with examples) as follows: (1) *bacterial,* as anthrax, blackleg, tuberculosis; (2) *virus-caused,* as cholera, rabies, fowlpox, foot-and-mouth; (3) *protozoan,* as gall sickness, malaria; (4) *worm parasites,* as tapeworm, trichinosis, hookworm; and (5) *arthropod,* as scabies, mites, blowfly worms. The three causes of non-infectious animal ills are poor diet, chemical and other pesticide poisoning, and poisonous wild plants. Weak hereditary traits also lead to some illnesses.

Treatment and prevention: To keep animals free of diseases requires constant care. Clean housing and feeding come first. Prompt isolating of sick animals comes next. A major preventive is to inoculate all animals with immunizing serums. As examples, vaccinating of young hogs against cholera has been successful. The family pet dog can get regular shots to protect it from distemper and rabies. New drugs and antibiotics can work wonder cures for many sick animals. D. A. B.

Animal husbandry Animal husbandry is the science of raising farm animals. The main part of this science is the breeding of animals, although the care, feeding, and marketing are also important.

Farm animals provide numerous products for us. Among the most common ones are the foods such as milk, eggs, butter, cheese, lard, and meat. ADRENALIN, pancreatin, INSULIN, pepsin, and thyroid extract are products derived from animals that benefit sick people. By-products from these animals also provide leather, glue, gelatine, wool, fertilizers, and tallow for soaps and candles.

A farmer in the livestock business has many problems raising his animals. Feeding can present a large problem. Cattle cannot be turned loose in a pasture and still get all the foods they require. They must be fed the proper grains at the proper time. Certain feeds will be required for health as well as for weight gain. Since cattle, hogs, sheep, and several other animals are sold according to their weight, proper weight gain is important to the farmer who has spent a good deal of his time and money raising these animals.

Good conditions, especially good grazing land, are important for cattle

Courtesy Society For Visual Education, Inc.

Living quarters for animals provide more problems and expenses for the farmer. Hogs cannot be left to wallow in the mud, and cattle cannot be left in pastures during all kinds of weather. These animals all require clean dry places with light and ventilation. Poultry animals must be protected against mice, rats, snakes, and other wild animals that disturb them. Dairy cattle farmers also must invest in a good deal of equipment that requires care and cleanliness, such as milking machines and coolers.

Diseases are a big threat to animal farmers because they may wipe out an entire flock or herd that has been costly. Many animals must be inoculated against disease. Others must be fed antibiotics and other medicines with their regular feed.

Farm animals are bred not only to produce a continuous source of new offspring, but also to improve the present breeds so they may survive in different climates, be more resistant to disease, and gain weight at a more rapid rate. J. D. B.

SEE ALSO: ANIMAL DISEASE, DAIRY PRODUCTS, FOWL, VETERINARY MEDICINE

Animal intelligence Many animals can learn. Even an earthworm can be taught to avoid electric shocks. Chickens learn to peck at only good-tasting objects. Dogs can be trained to guard and guide as in the cases of police dogs, war dogs, and seeing-eye dogs. Many animals are taught to perform in circuses, on the stage, and on television. Ham, the chimpanzee who rode in the rocket shot into space by the United States, learned how to press buttons to operate a camera and a tape recorder in the missile cone.

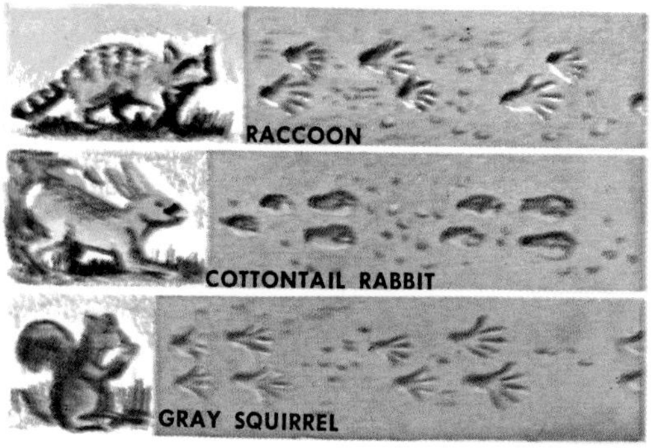

For centuries, man has been interested in the intelligence of animals. Back in the Middle Ages, there were two groups of thought on this question. One group said that animals were purely instinctive creatures with only the necessary powers of meeting life's demands—lacking will, purpose and reasoning ability. The other group stated that intelligence, or learned behavior, in addition to instinct, is present in lower animals as well as man.

Not until the last century with the work of DARWIN, Wallace and their fellow workers did we have reliable results concerning the evolution of intelligence in animals.

From 1860 on, the science of animal behavior has given us valuable facts about animal intelligence directly from experimental observation and scientific study, instead of relying on stories of intelligent acts performed by animals.

Emotions, such as fear, anger, startledness, pain and pleasure are being studied experimentally today in animals as they have been discussed for years in man. Although behavior is still an infant science, it has given scientists a great advantage in understanding intelligence, because experiments, especially in the lower animals, can be controlled. Many of these experiments would be extremely difficult or impossible with human subjects. J. K. K.

SEE ALSO: GENETICS

Animal tracks Animal tracks are marks left by an animal who has passed by. Many shy animals and those active by night are not often seen. Their presence is known by the tracks they leave on the ground. Woodsmen learn to recognize the footprints of different animals.

Other signs of a mammal's presence are gnaw marks, clipped twigs, scratchings, and scats (digestive wastes). Together with footprints they tell a story about the animals that made them.

Tracks of an animal vary with the kind of ground trod upon. Tracks in mud, snow, or dust are not exactly alike. Speed of locomotion also changes the appearance of tracks. Walking or running gaits show different footprint patterns. The whole foot may not make a complete print in a running gait. J. C. K.

✳ **THINGS TO DO**

WHAT ANIMAL LEFT THAT TRACK?

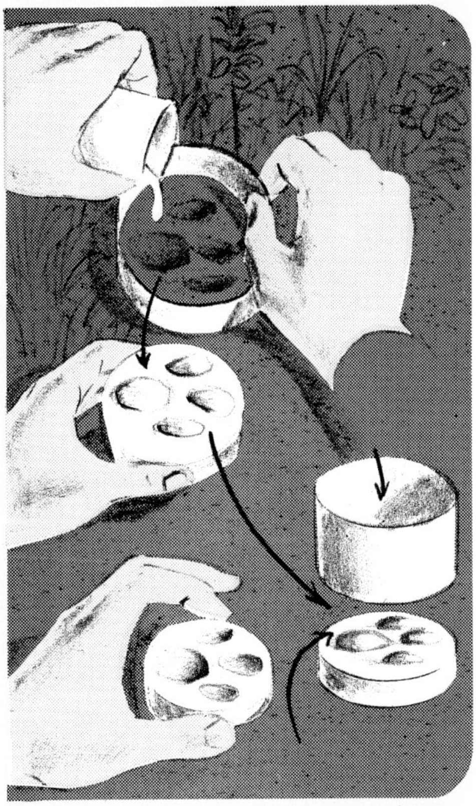

Materials: small sack of plaster-of-paris, can of water, spoon, cardboard cylinders

1 **Take a hike to the woods carrying the materials named.**
2 **When a footprint of some animal is discovered on the ground, place the cylinder of cardboard around it.**
3 **Mix some water in the plaster-of-paris to the consistency of pudding. Pour this mixture over the animal track and permit the material to harden.**
4 **Remove the mold, clean off the soil and grease the raised print with petroleum jelly. This is a negative print.**
5 **Place another circle of cardboard around the mold so that it extends a little above the level of the negative print.**
6 **Pour another mixture of plaster-of-paris on top of the first mold. When this hardens, separate the two pieces.**
7 **The second casting is a positive print (depression) of the animal's footprint.**

Animals, classification of We give animals scientific names, but in a different way than we name people. The name of one animal shows its *kind,* the group to which it belongs. The name of your pet house cat is *Felis domesticus. Felis* is a name shared by all cats—lions, tigers, all of our pet cats, and others. The name *domesticus* is shared by all house cats. A pet cat can also have a name like Whiskers or Inky which you give him, but, like your own first name, it means only him and not the group to which he belongs. Few lions have pet names, unless they live in zoos or circuses, but every lion has the name *Felis leo.*

Scientists separate animals because of their differences and put them into groups because of their likenesses. This is called *classification.* Animals have close relatives and distant relatives. The pet cat next door is more closely related to your pet cat than to any lion in Africa. The lion is a distant relative of your pet cat and of the cat next door.

Scientists call all living men (Negroes, orientals, whites and so forth) *Homo sapiens.* Tribes and nations are social groupings and not biological. In his biological grouping, man is related to the other members of the animal kingdom. His closest relatives are the apes and monkeys.

A person could spend his entire life in finding and counting all of the live animals in the world. He might never finish, however, because there are about one million different kinds of animals. Some are large enough for people to see. Some are too small to be seen except under a microscope. Many animals are hard to find because they live in the soil, in deep ocean water and in the bodies of other animals. Each year, many hundreds of new animals are discovered and added to the animal kingdom. The animals that are alike are grouped together in a system of classification.

EVOLUTION — BASIS FOR CLASSIFICATION

Few people are able to trace their ancestors of one thousand years ago. Scientists are interested in tracing ancestors of millions of years ago. By tracing the development of animal ancestors, animal relationships of today can be figured out. This kind of classification is based on *evolution.*

After studying and classifying animals, most scientists think that the first animals were one-celled, aquatic animals, similar to a protozoan. Some animals gradually adapted themselves to a new way of living. They left the water to live on land and a few of these left the land and moved through the air. As animals became pioneers in new ways of living, they needed more cells. Gradually, *specialized* cells developed to take care of special activities. Some animals remained one-celled. Others developed many cells and are called *multi-cellular* animals. These multicellular animals have evolved into thousands of species.

Many animals which possess structures helpful in correctly classifying animals are extinct, that is, they are no longer alive as a species. Those who study FOSSILS, paleontologists, have given important information about such animals as dinosaurs and trilobites which once lived in great numbers but now can be seen only when they are discovered as fossils. The knowledge of such animals, when they lived, and their plan of organization, have made the relationships between animals more clear.

Animals have been divided into about 25 large groups, called *phyla.* Some of these phyla include rare animals, seldom seen by man. The animals within one phylum may live in different parts of the world. They may differ in size, shape and color. Their living habits and their means of locomotion may differ. However, they are similar in basic structure. For example, the fish, the snake, and the monkey are found in the same subphylum because all possess a skeletal backbone of vertebrae for bodily support.

Phyla are broken down into *classes.* Classes are divided into groups called *orders.* Orders are further divided into different *families.* Families are divided into *genera* (singular: *genus*). Finally, genera are divided into *species.* The species is what most people refer to as a *kind* of animal. Each known species of animal has been given a proper scientific name. The correct scientific name is the name of the genus followed by the name of the species. The names are in Latin and are recognized by all scientists in the world.

To show how classification works, the scientific names of three familiar animals, the salmon, the lion, and the common house cat, can be traced. All are members of the phylum *Chordata* because they have supportive rods (notochords) sometime during life. The salmon is a member of the class *Osteichythes* because it is cold-blooded, breathes by means of gills, and deposits its eggs in the water. The salmon is classified as follows:

Phylum Chordata
Class Osteichythes
Order Teleostei
Family Salmonidae
Genus Oncorhynchus
Species tschawytscha

The scientific name of the quinnat salmon is *Oncorhynchus tschawytscha.*

The lion is a member of the Class *Mammalia* because it is warm-blooded, breathes by means of lungs, and nurses its young with milk. If the lion is traced in classification down to the species, it is found to be:

Phylum Chordata
Class Mammalia
Order Carnivora
Family Felidae
Genus Felis
Species leo

The lion's scientific name is *Felis leo.* The common house cat and the lion are very closely related. They are both of the cat family *(Felidae)* and of the genus *Felis.* Only their species are different. The house cat is of species *catus* (or *domestica*). When people see a house cat, not many think of its scientific names, *Felis catus,* or see the whole history of evolution behind the friendly cat, or its wild relative, the lion.

MAJOR PHYLA OF ANIMAL LIFE

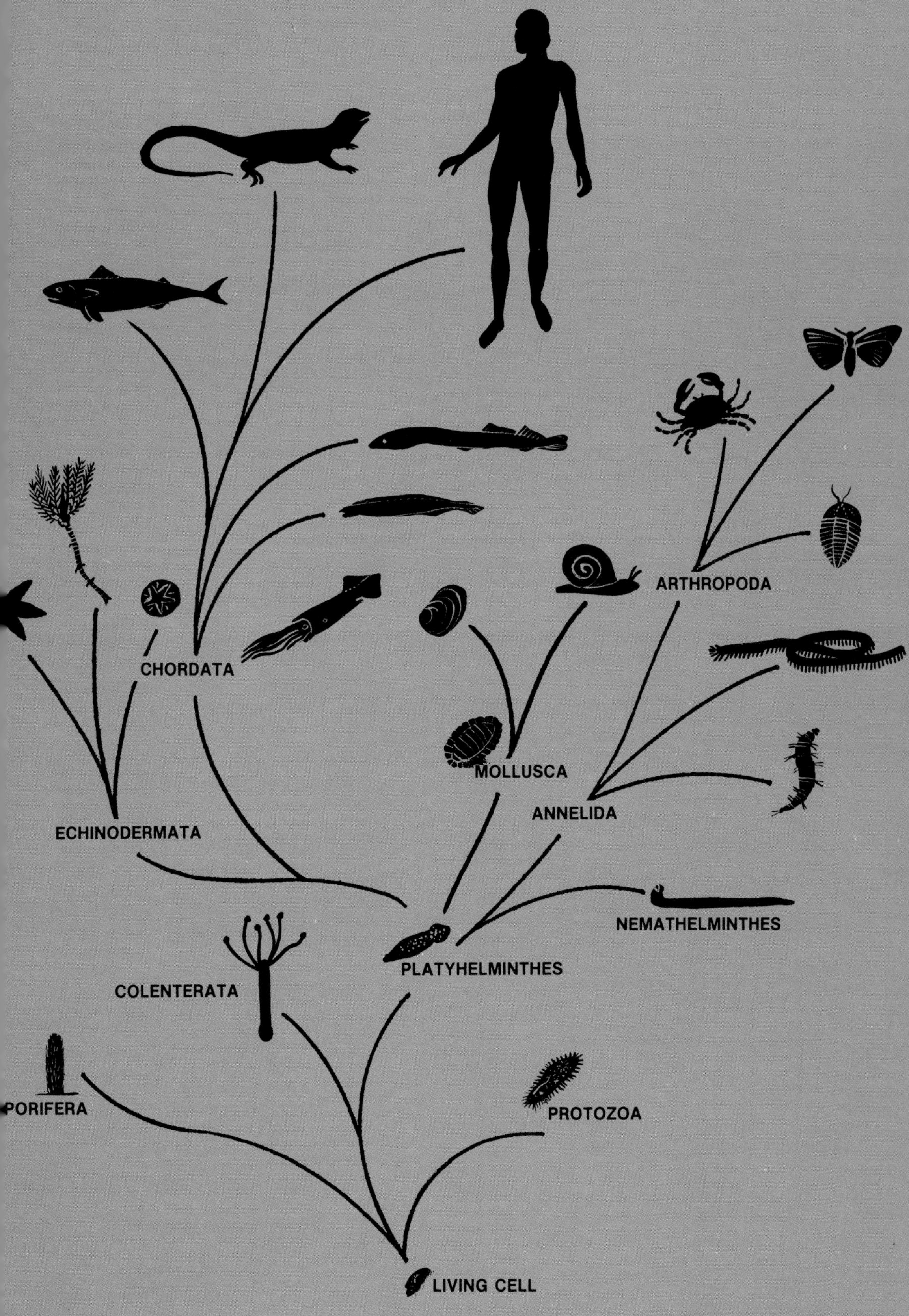

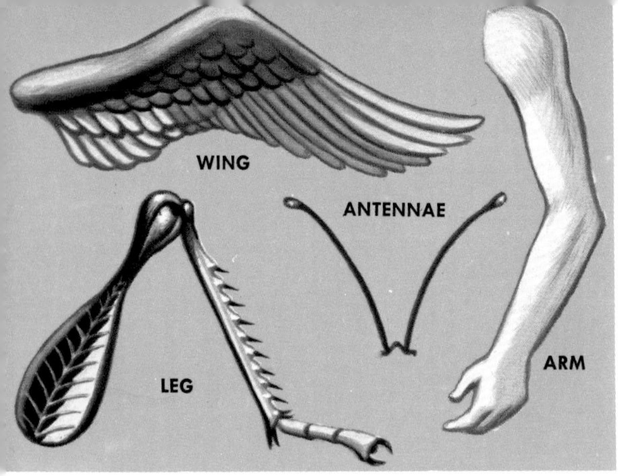

These structures are all appendages but only the arm and wing are homologous

GROUPING BY STRUCTURE

In order to understand animals and how they are related, a scientist must know how animals are built. He must know their shapes. He must know how they start to grow and how they change as they grow. He must know how the animal is constructed, both inside and outside.

It is important to know the inner structures because the outer structures can be deceptive. A GRASSHOPPER and CANARY may appear to be related. Both have wings which allow movement through the air, both have legs for movement on the ground, and both are streamlined in appearance. But a scientist, after closely observing the two animals, would find that the grasshopper breathed by means of hollow tubes or *trachea* and that it had an outer skeleton of chitin. He would also know that the canary breathed by means of lungs and that it had an inner skeleton of bone. The grasshopper is more closely related to the lobster. The canary is a bird and is more closely related to the frog. Scientists are able to make these judgments concerning animal structure because of the system they have developed for organizing the information about animals.

When animals have structures that are alike in ancestral origin, these structures are said to be *homologous* and provide a common relationship. The front fins of a fish and the wings of a bird are homologous. However, when structures of animals seem to be used for the same function but are of different ancestral origin, these structures are merely *analogous* and do not support placing these animals within the same group. The wings of an insect and the wings of a bird are analogous.

GROUPING BY EMBRYONIC DEVELOPMENT

The period of time during which the animal grows from a fertilized egg to a whole new animal is called the *embryonic period.* The animal is an embryo. Early in the course of embryonic development of higher animals, the fertilized egg divides into many cells. The cells become specialized and the animal grows into the familiar shape.

In some animals such as the frog, the embryo comes out as a free-living LARVA. The larval stage is a period of development between the embryonic and adult stages. For example, the tadpole is a larva, the frog is the adult. Eventually the larva goes through a change, or metamorphosis, and develops into an adult. Not all animals pass through the larval stage. Many, such as the bird and the human develop gradually into adults.

Scientists observe the development of both the embryo and the larva. They compare these developments with those of other animals. Some animals have similar embryos and similar larvae, even though the adults are entirely different. Development of the animal, from conception to adulthood, is important in classification.

GROUPING BY BODY FORM

Most animals have an axis, just as the Earth has an imaginary line, or axis, extending from the south to the north pole. The horse and the worm move along the ground in such a way that a line drawn along the back is horizontal to the ground. Animals like the ape and man move in such a way that the head becomes the highest point on the body. These animals have a *vertical* axis.

Animals have bodies which are organized according to a definite plan. A dividing line through the axis will divide most animals into similar or equal parts. For example, if a dog were divided along the main axis from head to tail, there would be a right side which looked almost exactly like the left side. A dog has *bilateral symmetry,* meaning that it has two similar sides which balance the body. Most land animals and many complex aquatic animals, like the fish and the squid, have bilateral symmetry. This allows for greater speed in moving through both air and water.

Many of the slow moving (or *sedentary*) aquatic animals, such as the coral, jelly fish, starfish, or sea urchin have another kind of symmetry, called *radial symmetry.* They have a vertical axis. Radial animals may be divided through the central, vertical axis into several equal parts, just as a round cake may be divided into many equal pieces of cake. HYDRA may be divided into many sections, each section containing a piece of the body and long tentacles. Radial animals either drift with the current or attach themselves to the ground. They are slow moving and less able to escape from their enemies.

A few members of the Protozoa, such as the radiolarians, are round like a ball. They have *spherical symmetry* because there is no main axis. Like a ball, they may be divided through the center into many equal sections. Some animals, like the ameba, have no definite axis, since they move into different shapes. They are *asymmetrical,* or lack symmetry.

GROUPING BY BODY SUPPORT

All animals need to be held together, otherwise, they would fall apart into lumps of jelly. Just as a building is held together with steel beams and cement blocks, an animal is held in shape with bones, muscles and CONNECTIVE TISSUE.

Muscles provide support for movement of the body. Unicellular and simple multicellular animals, such as the sponge and JELLY FISH contain tiny protein *fibrils* within cells. These fibrils contract and produce movements. More advanced animals have special MUSCLE TISSUE. In mammals, two-thirds of the body weight consists of muscle. Muscles can give support, move the skeleton, and maintain or change the shape of organs or the body as a whole.

A skeleton may consist of organic substances, such as CHITIN or spongin; or inorganic substances, such as calcium or silicon salts; or a combination of both, as in

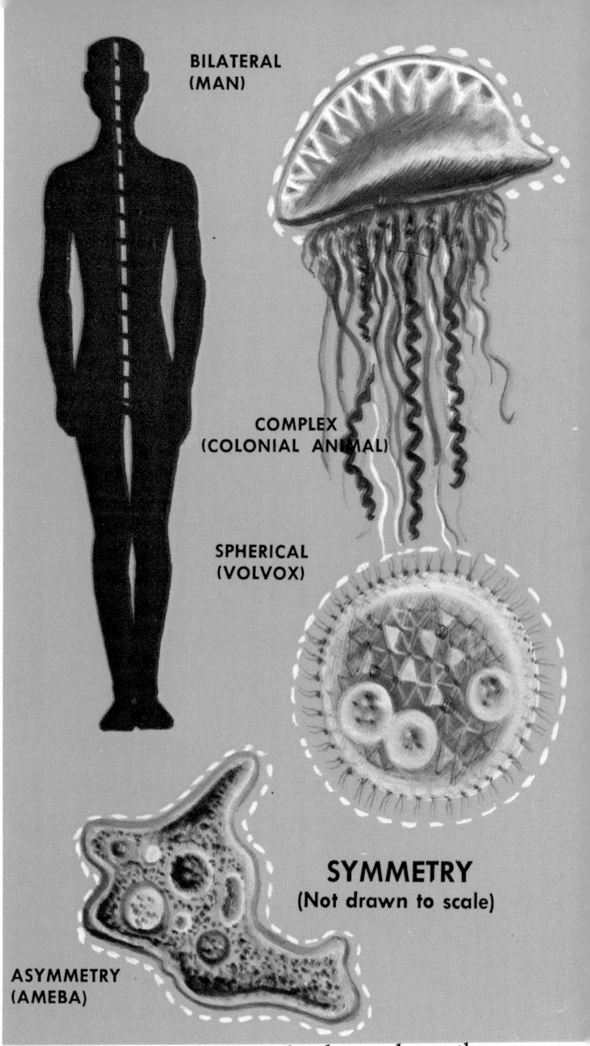

SYMMETRY
(Not drawn to scale)

bone. The skeleton may be located on the outside of the body, where it offers both support to soft inner tissues and protection against the outside environment. The shells of LOBSTER and the OYSTER and the chitinous covering of the BEETLE are examples of outer skeletons or *exoskeletons.* The skeleton may be located on the inside of the body where it offers support and protection to the inner tissues. The bony skeleton of the fish and the dog are examples of inner skeletons or *endoskeletons.*

Animals with a spinal column are called vertebrates. All vertebrates are grouped into a phylum called *Chordata.* Lower chordates, such as the lamprey, have a *notochord* or rod of cartilage, extending along the dorsal surface. Higher chordates, such as the bird and mammal, have skeletons of cartilage and bone. Since bone permits greater size, these animals have developed other complex organ systems, such as the circulatory system. Animals of all other phyla are called *invertebrates* because they do not possess a backbone. The type of body support is a basis for classification.

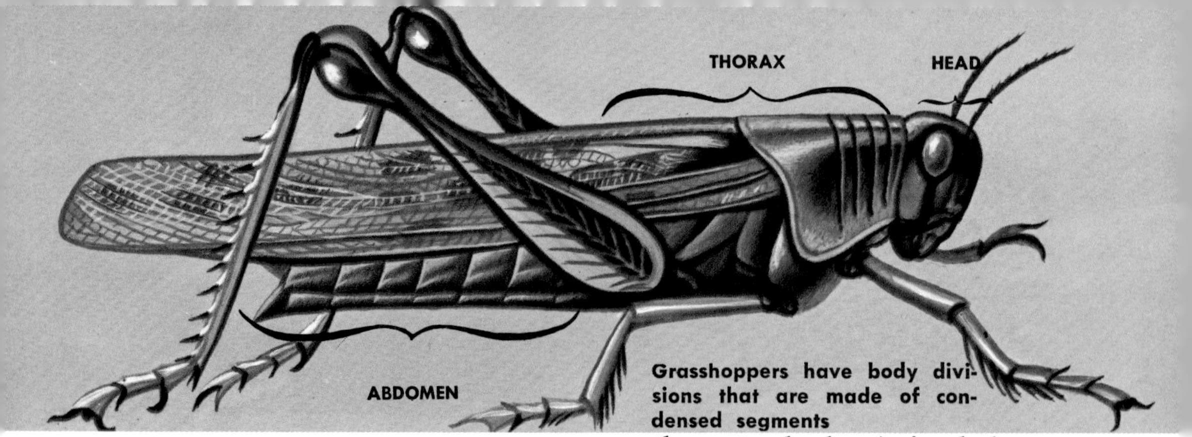

Grasshoppers have body divisions that are made of condensed segments

GROUPING BY SEGMENTATION

A tall building consists of separate floors which are joined together. Each floor is a complete unit. Some animals are constructed in sections. The sections of an animal body are called *metameres* or *segments* and are divided from each other by thin membranes. In some animals like the earthworm, the segments are alike and each segment contains similar organs. In the more advanced animals, such as the arthropods and the chordates, the segments fuse together to form definite body regions.

The front segments may be condensed to form the *head,* the middle segments condense to form the *thorax,* and the back segments condense to form the ABDOMEN. The original segments are not always visible on the outer surface of the animal.

The head is usually at the front, or anterior end, or at the highest point on the body, as is characteristic of the bird which stands on its hind legs. Sensory and feeding organs are located on the head. The thorax is between the head and abdomen. The arthropods have a thorax consisting of three or four fused segments. Insects may have a pair of wings on the last two segments. The thorax in mammals is a division of the body behind the neck. It consists of the thoracic cavity supported by the ribs, and separated internally by a DIAPHRAGM. The abdomen is the last division of the body. In some animals, it contains the anal and reproductive openings. Body divisions are a basis for classification.

GROUPING BY APPENDAGES

An appendage is an extra structure. It may be attached to an organ of the inner body or it may be attached to the outer body. Animals have appendages which serve for locomotion, perception, feeding, and defense.

There are many different types of appendages for locomotion. The one-celled animals may have cilia, flagella or pseudopodia. The arthropods and chordates have jointed appendages which are specialized for swimming, walking, running and jumping. Jointed appendages consist of a series of segments connected with each other and with the body. They are operated like levers by powerful muscles. Examples of jointed appendages are found in the wings of birds, the arms of man, the fins of fish and the legs of insects.

For the securing of food, the coelenterates and the mollusks have tentacles and cilia, the arthropods have mouth parts for sucking and tearing, and legs for grasping. For the purpose of defense, some animals possess tentacles, tails and poison glands. For exploration of the environment, the antennae or palpi of insects, the eyes, the nose and the ears of higher animals, serve as sensory organs. The types of appendages are a basis for classification.

GROUPING BY PHYSIOLOGY

Although it it more difficult to determine how animals are alike in function of parts than it is to compare their structure, sometimes studying the PHYSIOLOGY of animals is the only way to discover important relationships. As the science of comparative physiology progresses, the classification of animals will be made clearer.

After collecting much information on a particular animal, the scientists are prepared to compare it with others. Having made careful comparison, they are able to place the animal in the proper phylum with animals possessing similar structures. E.P.L.

SEE ALSO: ANIMAL, CELL, EMBRYOLOGY, EVOLUTION, METAMORPHOSIS, MUSCLE SYSTEM, PALEONTOLOGY, SKELETON, THE INDIVIDUAL PHYLA NAMES

Animals, life span Each different kind of animal has a different length of life. Scientists do not know why some animals live longer than others. The May fly will live only a few hours but a giant TURTLE is not old until it has lived more than a hundred years.

Scientists have discovered that the faster a living thing grows and the more active it is during its life time, the shorter its life will be. They say that each different kind of animal will seldom live longer than its parents lived. They know also that larger animals live longer than small ones and that animals having many offspring do not live as long as those having only a few. Animals that have a long GESTATION PERIOD (period of growth before birth) will live longer than those having a short period of gestation. These are all general rules and they do not apply to every species.

GRASSHOPPERS will live only a few months. They hatch out in the spring and die before cold weather comes. A grasshopper six months old is an old one, but a dog six months old is still a puppy. A dog is not considered old until he is about 12 years old. It is commonly thought that elephants live for a very long time. However, a sixty-year-old elephant is really old.

Some big tortoises, or turtles, live to be well over a hundred years. Turtles live longer than any other backboned animal (vertebrate). One that was in captivity lived to be 152 years old and even then he might have lived longer except that he was killed by accident. The common box turtle, which is a native of the United States, lives more than a hundred years. Man has a much longer life span than before, gained through control of disease. Except for certain species of turtles, not many animals live to be older than the oldest people.

Disease and other natural enemies cause shorter life of individual animals and of entire herds or flocks. An infectious disease may strike a herd of cattle and wipe out the whole herd. Improving the environment and controlling disease and natural enemies are good ways of increasing the length of life of animals.

In the animal world, there is a group of tiny one-celled animals which reproduce by dividing in two by fission. These are the PROTOZOA. Under the best environmental conditions, the life-span of the individuals may be short because they undergo fission rapidly. Crowding, lack of food or oxygen, accumulation of wastes, extremes of temperature are factors which act to gradually slow down the rate of fission. As the rate of fission decreases, the life-span of the individual organism may increase. However, when the effects of these factors become too extreme the environment is too poor to support life. The organisms will die or encyst. J. K. K.

SEE ALSO: AGING

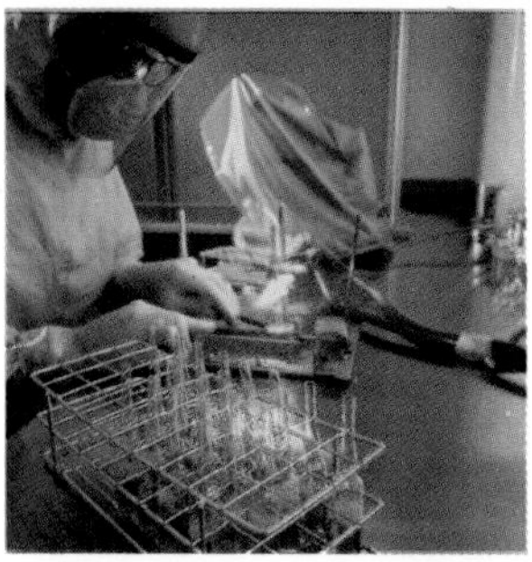

Conversion Factors to Metric Measurement

Length

1 inch = 25.4 millimeters (mm) exactly
1 inch = 2.54 centimeters (cm) exactly
1 foot = 0.3048 meters (m) exactly
1 yard = 0.9144 meters (m) exactly
1 mile = 1.609344 kilometers (km) exactly

Area

1 square inch = 6.4516 square centimeters (cm^2) exactly
1 square foot = 0.092903 square meters (m^2)
1 square yard = 0.836127 square meters (m^2)
1 square acre = 0.404686 hectares (ha)
1 square mile = 2.58999 square kilometers (km^2)

Cubic Measure

1 cubic inch = 16.387064 cubic centimeters (cm^3) exactly
1 cubic foot = 0.0283168 cubic meters (m^3)
1 cubic yard = 0.764555 cubic meters (m^3)

US Liquid Measure

1 fluid ounce = 29.5735 milliliters (ml)
1 fluid ounce = 0.2957 deciliters (dl)
1 pint = 0.473176 liters (l)
1 gallon = 3.78541 liters (l)

US Dry Measure

1 pint = 0.550610 liters (l)
1 bushel = 35.2391 liters (l)

Weight

1 grain = 0.0647989 grams (g)
1 ounce = 28.3495 grams (g)
1 pound = 0.453592 kilograms (kg)
1 short ton = 0.907185 metric tons (t)
1 UK ton = 1.01605 metric tons (t)

Temperature

To convert Fahrenheit to Centigrade complete the following equation.

$(F^\circ - 32) \times 5 \div 9 = C^\circ$